IN MY FATHER'S HOUSE ARE MANY MANSIONS

SAINT JULIAN PRESS

IN MY FATHER'S HOUSE ARE MANY MANSIONS

Thoughts & Sermons

By

Robert Paul Starbuck
MDiv, PhD

Saint Julian Press
Houston

Published by

SAINT JULIAN PRESS, Inc.
2053 Cortlandt, Suite 200
Houston, Texas 77008

www.saintjulianpress.com

COPYRIGHT © 2018
TWO THOUSAND AND EIGHTEEN
© Saint Julian Press, Inc.
EDITED BY RON STARBUCK

ISBN-13: 978-1-7320542-2-6
ISBN: 1-7320542-2-3
Library of Congress Control Number: 2018911041

Cover Art: *St. John Lutheran Church* – Easton, Kansas
Original Photograph by Kelly Mailen
Cover Design: Ron Starbuck
Author's Photo Credit: Family Archives

To my wife Edna Katerina Meinert Starbuck and our children, their spouses, our grandchildren, great grandchildren, and all the future generations of our family and humankind. This is the legacy I leave behind for you to keep safe and share.

~ Robert Paul Starbuck ~

JOHN 14:1-4 Authorized King James Version (AKJV)

14 Let not your heart be troubled: ye believe in God, believe also in me. ² In my Father's house are many mansions: if *it were* not *so*, I would have told you. I go to prepare a place for you. ³ And if I go and prepare a place for you, I will come again, and receive you unto myself; that where I am, *there* ye may be also. ⁴ And whither I go ye know, and the way ye know.

CONTENTS

THE MISSILES OF OCTOBER 1962	1
THE FUTURE OF HUMANKIND	3
MAN'S NEED – MORE THAN SURVIVAL	10
A NATION WEEPS	19
SOMETHING MORE THAN PALMS	25
YOU'VE GOT TO BE CAREFULLY TAUGHT	37
SOMETHING MORE IMPORTANT	43
DO YOU SEE WHAT I SEE?	49
THE AFTERGLOW	55
THE QUEST BELONGS TO EACH OF US	60
TO LIVE IS TO LOVE	66
WHAT IS TRUTH	72
WATCH FOR PLATFORM 9 3/4	77
GOD ABOVE GOD	83
AGAIN – FOR THE FIRST TIME	93
EVERLASTING LIFE – A PARADIGM SHIFT	100
LET MY PEOPLE GO	106

FOREWORD

Executive Editor – Saint Julian Press – Ron Starbuck

In a time of cultural wars, social polarizations, fears, conflicts, chaos, and once again the rise of nationalism, authoritarian ideologies and isolationism across the globe, there are questions we must ask ourselves as human beings. That is what this book does, as it also touches on the story of a generation who came before us. This is *"The Greatest Generation"* who lived through World War II, who stood up for justice and mercy. And who fought against many of the veiled and evil –"isms" inflicted upon humankind in the 20th and now in the 21st century.

American poet and the 9th Librarian of Congress, Archibald MacLeish wrote these verses in his seventh book of poetry, *The Hamlet of A.MacLeish* – published in 1928.

> "We have learned the answers, all the answers:
> It is the question that we do not know.
> We are not wise."

As an ordained United Methodist minister for over fifty-five years, and practicing psychotherapist for over forty years, our father — the Rev. Dr. Robert P. Starbuck — never read the Bible in a literal way. It was always a quest, a quest which belongs to each of us, to ask the right questions. As clergy, he saw the beloved Bible stories, readings, and lessons, as a way of wisdom. As a way of being and becoming; a way of forgiveness, renewal, redemption, reconciliation, salvation and spiritual enlightenment. In his calling as a minister and therapist, he was actively engaged in the lives of others, and in healing and repairing the world.

He saw the Bible stories as something to be taught, cherished, and celebrated as sacred literature and scripture, as poetic and symbolic language. Our beloved stories of the Bible are filled with wonderful allegories and metaphors, pointing humankind towards a higher truth and experience of the divine. A way that points us towards an intimate and eternal relationship with the divine that is ours to claim, a new being and a new creation. As a minister he believed in and administered the Holy Sacraments of the church. He believed in the Ultimate Divine Mystery, the "Real Presence" of Christ, and of the Holy Spirit – the Love of God, actively at work within the world today. Bringing people together!

He was able to live in this mystery, to accept it fully and completely, and came to realize early in his adult life what Jesus was ultimately teaching humankind. Not to judge others, but to love God and others as yourself – the "Golden Rule" in many faiths. We find this in the two greatest commandments of Christ.

> *Hear what our Lord Jesus saith:*
>
> *Thou shalt love the Lord thy God with all thy heart, and with all thy soul, and with all thy mind. This is the first and great commandment. And the second is like unto it: Thou shalt love thy neighbor as thyself. On these two commandments hang all the Law and the Prophets. Matthew 22:37-40*

In his ministry, he urged people to embrace life, to live their lives in great spiritual abundance and fullness, without separation, wholly *(holy)* aware and completely open – alive with wonder. He believed in Jesus Christ and the message and gift of God's love and acceptance for humanity, of salvation and oneness within the Trinity. He saw these as divine mysteries that take us beyond all faiths, religious beliefs, doctrines and dogmas, symbols, words, and images. He saw God as something more. Spirit and Truth.

He believed in the unity of God's Spirit, the Holy Spirit, unseen and invisible that is always waiting for us to claim the power of God's love and healing within our own lives. And he believed in the transforming power of God's love, God as love and Christ as God's love made manifest within the world. In the end, this work is an affirmation of his faith.

IN MY FATHER'S HOUSE ARE MANY MANSIONS

THE MISSILES OF OCTOBER 1962

An Introduction

"FOR THIRTEEN DAYS in October 1962, the world waited — seemingly on the brink of nuclear war — and hoped for a peaceful resolution to the Cuban Missile Crisis." — John F. Kennedy Presidential Library & Museum

THESE TWO SERMONS are a response to what was going on in America and the world at this moment in history. Each one is a slice of history. You may wish to explore that history and its impact on humanity more on your own. The events are well known now.

Eight months later, in June 1963, President Kennedy offered Americans the following words: "For, in the final analysis, our most basic common link is that we all inhabit this small planet. We all breathe the same air. We all cherish our children's future. And we are all mortal."

It may be helpful to remember that President Kennedy was the first Roman Catholic to hold the office, much as President Obama was the first African American to hold the office for two terms.

In the midst of the Cuban Missile Crisis, you will find two sermons. One is a call for an ecumenical dialogue between Protestants and Catholics, between fellow Christians. Let this theme of reformation serve as a poetic allusion — a symbolic reflection of what was happening between two nations of the world then and now. The second is seeking peace in a world wavering on the edge of nuclear destruction.

They could apply equally to America today, across the chasm of ideologies and politics that separate us. Our ideologies have become like idols, graven images, inflexible and cold, without warmth or love or compassion for our fellow human being. It is far from the "Peace of Christ," and the peace of God, which surpasses all understanding, and the peace and future of a nation and the world. There are times when all sides, must set aside their differences for the peace and welfare of the world. This was true then, and it is the same today, as we face new and critical challenges on a global scale.

In the years that followed the events of October 1962. The world began to see a radical openness take shape in the context of an interfaith dialogue. That dialogue continues today, in new and wondrous ways and in cross–cultural and interfaith spiritual practices. Even as we hold on to and cherish the traditions and liturgy of our core faith, the faith of our fathers and mothers. Humanity may also learn new ways to pray, interact, and inter-relate with people of many different faiths as a family of humanity.

Many of us have perceived, or are beginning to envision — that the mystical — Real Presence of Christ, and the Holy Spirit are actively at work within the world. We see this happening as we witness God's interconnecting spirit, love, and compassion — flowing through all the faiths and people of humankind. As an affirmation of many faiths, reformation and reconciliation in this sense take on new meanings in the affairs of humankind. There is a new evangelism at work within Christianity grounded in an interfaith dialogue. From this thought and an open dialogue across humanity's many faiths came forth the book's title — *In My Father's House Are Many Mansions*.

Ron Starbuck – Executive Editor – Saint Julian Press

THE MISSILES OF OCTOBER 1962 – THE FUTURE OF HUMANKIND

October 28, 1962 – Reformation Sunday

"YOUR WORLD WAS A WORLD without hope and without God. But now in union with Christ Jesus you who once were far off have been brought near through the shedding of Christ's blood. For he is himself our peace...for he annulled the law with its rules and regulations, so as to create out of the two a single new humanity in himself, thereby making peace. This was his purpose, to reconcile the two in a single body to God through the cross, on which he killed the enmity (hatred)." – Ephesians 2:12-16 *(New English Bible)*

THIS IS OUR PURPOSE today as Christians and as Protestants. On this Reformation Sunday, we must remember that it is not only a day, which commemorates the martyrs whose blood was shed in testimony of their faith; it is a day of reform within our own lives. We must look back to that historical event known as the Protestant Reformation. We must see and become a part of that reformation which did not stop with Martin Luther but echoed down through the ages and vibrates with emotion as we hear and sing such words as;

> A mighty fortress is our God,
> A bulwark never failing;
> Our helper He, amid the flood
> Of mortal ills prevailing;
> For still our ancient foe
> Doth seek to work us woe
> His craft and power are great,
> And armed with cruel hate,
> On earth is not his equal.

The reformation is not merely a thing of the past or even of the present. It is a thing of the future — and its future, the future of your world and mine will depend upon our acceptance of Christ Jesus our Lord, and our belief that out of Him, a single new humanity is formed, in which everlasting peace and tranquility are found.

In a time when the world is threatened by total destruction. In a time when humanity is indifferent towards one another because of opposing ideologies and ways of life. In a time when hate is greater than love. We need to turn and to re-accept our humanity, which is our gift of power and our only hope for Life in the midst of death.

We need more than ever to set afresh the word Reformation — realizing that the significance of the word stems from its meaning to reform, to start life anew, to seek unity in the midst of disunity a unity needed for both the survival of Christianity and the world at large.

Americans, I fear are still blind to the fact that war, conflict, and chaos are no longer the answer to separation. War has always lost more than it has gained — its wounds are never really healed. Take, for example, our own nationhood.

More than one hundred years have passed, and the wounds of the Civil War still drain and smart with — fervor and emotions. The embittered feelings, the racial and partisan hatred evolving out of people of one nation penetrates our very being and cause us to wonder of our purpose as Christians.

So, it is in international affairs; even here the problem becomes of great magnitude and complexity. Nation against nation is a step above people against people. We think different. We believe different. Our goal is different.

We are unable to communicate because we speak different languages. We see only the sins and indifference of the other nation, and the mistrust, which we have toward one another. This is not to say that our present position is wrong, perhaps it is not! I do not know if it is.

I do not think President Kennedy, or any given member of our State Department, knows the answer — so one must merely feel his way as in the dark, hoping and praying as he moves along inch by inch, minute by the minute. I do not know the answer, do you, really?

I did see the hell of war; and the aftermath of WW II in Germany and France remains as a vivid memory for me — the crying of little children, the war-torn faces of widows and orphans, of old men and old women still has not lost its imprint in more than a decade and a half.

I am more mature now! At the age of eighteen, I couldn't wait—I had to see action; now nineteen years later and after the birth of four children, I'm not so anxious. I stop and think and pray. I look at both sides of the coin and war, conflict, and chaos are not the answer.

What is the answer? Peace—Love! This is what existence of the United Nations is proposing. This is what both Russia and the United States claim they want. Of course, we call Russia liar, and they call us warmonger and liars in return.

Certainly, there is more to be said than to say that we are right, and they are wrong. Oh, we want to say this, and we do because it sounds good. But we as a nation are not guiltless, and it was due primarily to our stupidity and our longing for a firmer economic foothold in Cuba that the Cuba reformation under Castro came into being.

I think we would have wanted a reform too if we had been living under the rule and exploitation of Dictator Batista. However, we supported him as a nation because of economic reasons only. We didn't, and I still don't think we really are concerned with Cuba as children of God. That is, I have a feeling that a greater concern is the re-establishment of economic relations.

This in no way excuses Russia; her massive infiltration and her continuous threat of communism the world over. It does, however, point the way to our sins and our means of manipulation in world affairs and international relations. To me, the United Nations is the one organization that can bring peace into the world.

You may have lost all faith in the likelihood even that a meeting of the minds, be it, a summit conference or a gathering with the Secretary-General of the U.N. can save the world from complete annihilation. You might agree with a former president when he said, "I don't believe in them, they don't amount to a damn. I have been to two of them and nothing was accomplished."

What end is it that we want to accomplish that a hydrogen bomb would accomplish? Acting United Nations Secretary General, U Thant, in a recent speech before the Security Council made this statement: "What is at stake is not just the interests of the parties directly involved, nor just the interests of all member states, but the very fate of humankind. If today the United Nations should prove itself ineffective, it may have proved itself so for all time."

Here a man of the Buddhist faith, outshines a Christian nation. While affirming his own faith he recognizes that there are hundreds and millions of people who believe otherwise. He says, "I understand this, and because of this understanding, I believe in peaceful co-existence."

Whether we like it or not, (he continues) "I believe that communism is going to stay; I believe capitalism is going to stay; I believe parliamentary democracy is going to stay...I believe the day will come when these different societies...are going to exist peacefully. I believe in these things."

I too believe in these things. As a Christian, I too believe that the world can be one even as Christ is one. That in the midst of distinct cultures and different races and faiths and minds, a thread of unity will shape the peace, and the world and humanity shall live in a universe of love and tranquility.

"This was his purpose, to reconcile the two in a single body to God through the cross, on which he killed the enmity (Hatred)." Ephesians 2:16 *(New English Bible)*

The Reformation — It's Future! I suppose that this brings us then to the heart of the message, the very core, if you please. For on this Reformation Sunday, we seek unity not only among the minds of nations and the world; we also strive towards unity among the minds of Christian leaders within the circle of the Church of Jesus Christ. We cannot help but recall the conflicts, which separates the Church on this day.

It certainly equals, may even excel the differences, which divided the Jewish Christians and the Gentile Christians in Paul's day. As Protestants, we know the difficulty that is ours in coming to some understanding with those teachings and principles of Roman Catholicism. The anti-Catholic feelings, which many of us have or have had in the past, deeply affect this wound of separation.

We forget in the given moment that we are Christian brothers and sisters to one of another. Our hatred and animosity inflame the whole self, and like cancer cells spread in all directions. We would rather be damned, then to sit at a table seeking the very unity, which destroyed not by God, but by humankind.

How strange it must seem to those who think in that direction that the leaders of Roman Catholicism and Protestantism are now seeking unity. This does, not mean that as Protestants. We can ever forget the history and cause of our separation.

But, is it also possible to agree on a unity of mission as servants? Even as we consider both our disparities and common ground such as (1) The Sacraments, (2) The Priesthood of all believers, (3) The freedom of mind and thought. Our separation may not be as great as we may well imagine.

Certainly, it is possible, to find such unity in the light of Christ Jesus our Lord — to live in peaceful accord. Striving at all times for the unity of one mind and heart, believing that this unity does' not come about by humankind's doings alone but by the spirit of God working in the lives of his children.

Accordingly, it seems to me that if unity is ever to come it must come via three directions. First, it must come via of the Church at Rome. In an opening statement at the Second Vatican Council – on October 11, 1962, Pope John XXIII furnished these words.

"The Catholic church, therefore, considers it her duty to work actively so that there may be fulfilled the great mystery of that unity, which Jesus Christ invoked with fervent prayer from His Heavenly Father on the eve of His sacrifice."

The results of this council will most likely not, furnish any momentous change in Christendom. The very fact that so large a body of Protestants is represented, shows for the first time a genuine concern on the part of a Catholic Pope for unity and peaceful co-existence.

Second, if unity is ever to come it must come also in the direction of Protestantism. Not only must our leaders be concerned with unity but we as members of the Faith must support them and be concerned ourselves with the separation. We must examine every way and mean, for such a oneness. If nothing more, we must be willing to envision this unity — recognizing our shared values and moving on from there.

You see people can live together although their minds think different, and their thoughts diverge in opposite directions. We have seen this within the family where one is Protestant and one is Catholic, or one is Christian one Jewish or Muslim or another faith.

Oh yes — you can quickly point out (if you must) those families who have failed under these conditions. I am speaking of those families who have learned to live and to love in spite of their differences. I think now of such families within our own church who confront this, but because of love, live in unity.

A year ago, the Third Assembly of the World Council of Churches, the Protestantism voice was heard, in her message flow these convictions. "We must together seek the fullness of Christian unity.

Our brethren in Christ are given to us, not chosen by us. In some things, our convictions; do not yet permit us to act together. However, let us, everywhere find out the things which we can do now; and faithfully do them praying and working always for that fuller unity which Christ wills for his Church."

This brings us then to the fixed direction. If unity is ever to come between Protestants and Catholics or across all faiths, it must come via God. Only if we allow room in our discussion, our debate, and our arguments for the Holy Spirit to work, will our Unity be possible. It is not so much that we can bring it to pass; as we look at our diverse views, it frightens us, and we see chaos and further separation. Hence, the minds of humankind must be supported by a greater mind — one that knows no separation and longs for God's children to live in peace and unity.

In the same way, wise nations can be brought together. Even so, it requires a given trust in a world of mistrust, and it requires faith in the midst of doubt. As a Christian, I do not believe in war and conflict. Still, I believe that unity is possible only through the exchanges of human minds where the Holy Spirit has an opportunity to work in mysterious and miraculous ways.

Let us pray.

Sermon delivered at Valley View United Methodist Church in Overland Park, Kansas, on October 28, 1962.

THE MISSILES OF OCTOBER 1962 – HUMANITY'S NEED – MORE THAN SURVIVAL

November 11, 1962 — Veterans Day

IN AN EDITORIAL written for the *American Journal of Orthopsychiatry* and appearing in the January 1962 issue of that periodical, Dr. Margaret Mead quoted a statement by the World Federation for Mental Health: "For the first time in human history, men have come face to face with the possibility that mankind might be wiped out."

This fact has radically altered the whole position with regard to peace and war. The choice lies no longer in the bands of groups of individuals, of giving their lives willingly in order that liberty or justice, or freedom from hunger, may prevail, whether for themselves or for others. The dilemma now facing the world is essentially a matter of precipitating, or preventing... a world conflict from which, even though some might conceivably survive, none would live to inherit any possible spiritual or indeed, material, fruits of 'victory'."

Having just passed another crisis in world affairs, which brought us to the brink of war, it seems fitting on this Veteran's Day 1962, to look more closely at our need, to take time and see that need in light of the Gospel of Jesus Christ. This morning, I would like to have you look with me in three directions, first, to the world and the survival of the human race. Second, to one of the most talked about emotional topics of our day — Radioactive Fallout and Fallout Shelters — and third to the working hypothesis which I believe will not only solve our present dilemma but once again will set in motion the reconstruction of the human race into something more than mere survival.

First then, let us look to the world and the survival of the human, race, i.e., the existence of the world and the human race. What is it that keeps the world going, keeps it revolving around the sun every 24 hours? What is it that keeps our temperature at a livable degree? Surely, we are aware that a small shift, in the distance, between the earth and the sun could cause the earth either to freeze or burn up.

Likewise, an alteration in the ratio inside the body of salt to water, of oxygen to carbon dioxide, of red to white blood cells, could put an end to life. What is it that keeps our world, our race from destroying itself physiologically? The answer, of course, is equilibrium–balance, "Life is made possible by the most precarious balancing acts in the universe," writes Norman Cousins, editor of *Saturday Review*. In fact, we can say that the universe is likely made by a balancing creative force, which in its original nature was of a perfect nature. Humanity, so new to the "how's" of such a perfect creation does not know — this still remains a mystery to the human race.

We do know, however, that the world is set up in polarity and the only thing that keeps it intact is a balancing process. Heraclitus, an ancient Greek philosopher spoke wisely when he said, "Tension between opposites governed by a rational principle which holds them in balance is the key to the understanding of the world."

Might I add — that it is not only a key to the understanding of the world, but it is the key to the survival of the world! In like nature, Plato's whole philosophical system is set up in polarity and as one studies the Neo-platonic thought of form and matter, being and nonbeing — comparing this with Aristotle's two opposing factors: potentiality-actuality, humankind-God, humanity realizes the imminent danger of his own selves and their own world, which is now threatened by unbalance and unrest.

Certainly, we have felt this danger in the past two weeks. We have been threatened as never before with total destruction! I suppose the most startling thing in this entire episode —this whole possibility of final destruction lies in the fact that it comes not as natural means. Where we begin to see that the unbalancing of the universe may not come from the earth passing too near or far away from the sun; rather by the capacity that humanity now has to destroy life and the world at large.

The very God, who created the world in such an intrinsic way so that all things were in balance, now sees (as we see) his world threatened by those who think they can unbalance his nature and still live! No longer are we active in an age when we can give our lives in war for the survival of others, for even if they should endure they would have no spiritual or material fruits of victory. As Margaret Mead reiterated in her editorial, our choice is now one, of precipitating or preventing a world conflict. Our choice is no longer between war and peace, but war or peace-either we learn to live together, or we die together. This is our balance — this is our only hope!

Second, we need to turn our attention to one of the most sensitive topics of our day, radiation fallout and shelters. On November 1, 1961 Alton Blakeslee, Associated Press Science Writer, wrote an article entitled "Emotional Factors Are Extremely High in the Radioactive Fallout Problem."

He began his article with these words: "The scariest word of the day is fallout.... The odds are almost nothing that present amounts of fallout will hurt you as an individual. Still, it is equally true that some people somewhere will be damaged or will die too soon, possibly – ultimately thousands of people from fallouts already loosed by bomb tests... Bombs striking cities and missiles bases would suck up millions of tons of dirt, making it highly radioactive, carrying it perhaps 20 miles up. In an hour, it would start falling down, carpeting great areas with radioactivity..."

The next day he followed this article by saying, "The greatest toll from Russia's monster 50 megaton H-bomb could be among tomorrow's children. Its radioactive fallout might doom hundreds or even thousands of the world's children, over several future generations, to early death or physical or mental defects from hereditary damage. Many geneticists assume that any increase in radiation could cause genetic damage to some people...A National Academy of Sciences' committee has estimated 2 billion children will be born in the world during the next 30 years, and that some 4 million of them would possess tangible genetic effects from natural or spontaneous causes. Different authorities estimate 2 to 10 per cent of such genetic defects might be due to natural background radiation. So, even a slight increase in radioactivity produced by bomb tests could increase this rate of genetic mutations."

Of course, he ends his series of articles by saying, "A consensus of the experts; Bomb testing represents a definite but small hazard to human posterity." Yet, might we ask, as Christians is there any such thing as a small right or a small wrong to human posterity?

It is a Christian truth (is it not?) that we are all of us family to one another — we are responsible to the whole human race, not just part of it. When one of us sins, we are a part of that sin. We must accept the other person, without judgement, to the point of suffering with them in love and compassion because of their sin.

Then too, there are more to nuclear explosions than most of us want to think about. Norman Cousins, who has already been mentioned as the editor of *Saturday Review*, wrote a book entitled "*In Place of Folly*". It is a book dealing with the dangers of nuclear power in a world of international anarchy; as the publisher claims it is a message of hope, so long as "we do not crave the destruction of being the last generation of humans on earth."

According to the author, this is what happened at Hiroshima. The explosion produced a firestorm, the air swept in from all sides of the target area, whipping up the flames. As the heat rose, a vast canopy of smoke spread up and out. The result was a swirl of air, drawing in fresh air to excite and feed the fire. Even at the edge of the firestorm, winds of 40 miles an hour carried the blaze. The large number of frame houses added to the intensity of the fire. It is not necessary to speculate (he continues) on the effects of a hundred-megaton bomb.

Consider the power of a 10-megaton H-bomb…Brick and concrete buildings more than a few hundred feet from the center of the Hiroshima atomic explosions were not destroyed. In such an explosion, however, all brick structures would collapse within an area of more than 300 sq. miles. Private underground shelters would experience "Fall- in;" that is, a building and all the objects inside it would fall into the shelter…scorching winds from a 10-megaton bomb would deliver serious injury to people even on the outer fringes of a 2,000 square-mile area.

In the early years after Hiroshima, before the advent of both the hydrogen bomb and ballistic missile, the defense of cities was tied to evacuation procedures. Today, any mass evacuation is ruled out. Evacuation depends on adequate warning time; this no longer exists. A nuclear-tipped missile can now cross a large ocean in fifteen minutes or less. This then is why I mentioned shelters along with Radioactive Fallout. While I realize that fallout shelters may save some lives), I have a real fear within me that they are much less defensive than we are led to believe.

All information flowing from the experts in the field of science points to the need of better and more protective fallout shelters. On television, I recently heard that the Defensive Dept. of Greater Kansas City was concerned because people were not building more shelters; therefore, they were cutting the requirement in half, i.e., to the type and thickness of the shelter.

As I heard this, I thought to myself what is their motive? Is it really a concern for the survival of the human race?

Humanity's Need – More Than Survival! This I submit to you this morning as we explore together our third point or direction! It seems to me that the working hypothesis, which will solve our present dilemma and set in motion the reconciliation of the human race, must start within the individual.

It must start within your life and mine. I found in a recent article written by Dr. Paul Tillich, which I discovered in Tidings, a church paper of the Mt. Lebanon Methodist Church in Pittsburg, Pa., a note of relevancy. The article itself entitled "What is the meaning of life?"

It was based upon those fundamental questions of: Where do we come from, where do we go? What shall we do, what should we become in the short stretch between birth and death? In other words, humanity lives in an age where they are concerned with their existence, and humankind asks such questions about that existence! In fact, in Tillich's theology, he insists that humanity must ask before they can receive the answer.

Just as little children confront their parents with questions of their existence, so we as children of God confront Him with questions of our existence. The difficult, says Tillich, is that such questions are not answered or even asked if the "dimension of depth" is lost. And this is precisely what is wrong—human beings have lost the courage to ask with an infinite seriousness—as former generations did—and they has lost the courage to receive answers to these questions, wherever they may come from.

In our Scripture Lesson this morning the period of Israel's history was in the post-exile era. In her former days before her exile into

Babylon, she too had failed to ask the questions now under the rule of another people —with loss of freedom she has time to think.

Psalm 137 – Lament over the Destruction of Jerusalem

By the waters of Babylon,

there we sat down and wept,

   when we remembered Zion.

2 On the willows there

   we hung up our lyres.

3 For there our captors

   required of us songs,

and our tormentors, mirth, saying,

   "Sing us one of the songs of Zion!"

And she remembered Jerusalem—it was her highest joy! And truly the words coming from the 14th chapter of Hosea depict the response of God to his chosen people in this period fallowing' "the destruction of the nation Israel,

Hosea 14 – Assurance of Forgiveness

I will heal their faithlessness;

   I will love them freely,

     for my anger has turned from them.

5 I will be as the dew to Israel;

   he shall blossom as the lily,

   he shall strike root as the poplar;

> 6 his shoots shall spread out;
>
>> his beauty shall be like the olive,
>>
>> and his fragrance like Lebanon.
>
> 7 They shall return and dwell beneath my shadow,
>
>> they shall flourish as a garden;
>
> they shall blossom as the vine,
>
>> their fragrance shall be like the wine of Lebanon.

It is time that we realize that survival is not enough. Physically, we may live from day to day; even so, unless we take upon ourselves the courage to be and ask questions about our own existence, about our purpose and responsibility in the world. And then unless we have the courage to receive the answer, even though it hurts —unless we do this, we do not live, we do not have the kind of Life found in Christ Jesus our Lord.

If this morning, we accept seriously our Christian faith, we will go forth asking the question and through faith in Him whom we have come to worship, we will find the answer. We will know that we are nothing until this "something more," this mystery we call God becomes a part of our very being. As the author of our closing hymn wrote in the last verse:

MAKE ME A CAPTIVE, LORD

> My will is not my own
>
> Till Thou has made it Thine
>
> If it would reach a monarch's throne
>
> It must its crown resign.
>
> It only stands unbent

Amid the clashing strife,
When on thy bosom it has leant
And found in Thee its life.

Sermon delivered at Valley View United Methodist Church in Overland Park, Kansas, on November 11, 1962.

A NATION WEEPS

November 24, 1963 – The Assassination of John F. Kennedy

"FOUR SCORE and seven years ago our fathers brought forth on this continent, a new nation, conceived in Liberty, and dedicated to the proposition that all men are created equal.

Now we are engaged in a great civil war, testing whether that nation, or any nation so conceived and so dedicated, can long endure. We are met on a great battle-field of that war. We have come to dedicate a portion of that field, as a final resting place for those who here gave their lives that that nation might live. It is altogether fitting and proper that we should do this.

But, in a larger sense, we cannot dedicate—we cannot consecrate—we cannot hallow—this ground. The brave men, living and dead, who struggled here, have consecrated it, far above our poor power to add or detract. The world will little note, nor long remember what we say here, but it can never forget what they did here. It is for us the living, rather, to be dedicated here to the unfinished work which they who fought here have thus far so nobly advanced. It is rather for us to be here dedicated to the great task remaining before us -- that from these honored dead we take increased devotion to that cause for which they gave the last full measure of devotion -- that we here highly resolve that these dead shall not have died in vain -- that this nation, under God, shall have a new birth of freedom -- and that government of the people, by the people, for the people, shall not perish from the earth."

Abraham Lincoln
November 19, 1863

LITTLE DID I REALIZE — Thursday night as I looked upward toward the monumental face of Abraham Lincoln that I would be repeating this morning the words of his famous Gettysburg Address, which came to me at that time. I was more than 500 miles from where we stand now. I was walking along one of the streets of Louisville, KY. Suddenly, we came upon it — there it was, this monumental statue of Abraham Lincoln.

The spotlight was thrown on this face — black with the tarnish of time, as black as those people who he unchained, to whom he gave a new birth of freedom. Mysteriously, the feature of this statue depicted a man whose life was filled with love — love for humanity, for nation, love for God. It was like a magnet — pulling you upward until you found yourself present, with this man of history.

And there the words of history spoke softly to your listening ears: "Fourscore and seven years ago our fathers brought forth on this continent a new nation conceived in liberty and dedicated to the proposition that all men are created equal."

Tenderly I placed these words back into my subconscious where they had come from in this moment of encounter — I walked quietly onward towards the Sheraton Hotel where I was staying.

I had planned this morning to preach on the subject "The Unbalanced Diet" to point out the unbalance of our physical–spiritual life. The sermon died with the tragic death of our President at 1:00 PM Friday.

At the time, I was in a car driving back from Louisville. I did not hear the news immediately. It was not until we stopped in St. Louis at 1:35 (more than an hour after he was shot) that I learned the tragic news. It was in the Men's Room of the Ramada Inn, an employee, dressed in work clothes with tears in his eyes at the death of our President. It was a heavy blow to me as it was to everyone I came in contact with. The President of the United States of America was dead.

The President was killed by a man whose life was filled with hate. He did not hate the President or America; he hated himself. To say that he was a lover of Russia and the Communists and for this reason he killed, our president — are gullible and senseless words.

    He did not love Russia.

    How could he?

    He did not love himself.

His unstable mind may have favored Communist thinking, but he loved no one; for you cannot love one person and hate another — anymore than you love God and hate humanity.

Listening on our radio from St. Louis to Kansas City, we heard reporters from all over the world. While many of our stations in the early hours following his death were still playing "Rock-N-Roll" Europe was listening to funeral music. Their networks announced the news and immediately and switched from their regular program. Willy Brandt in West Berlin called upon his people to place a lighted candle in every window. The reporter from Moscow spoke these words: "A general condolence has been expressed by the Russian people."

All across the world, people were shocked at the word of the President's death. Here in America, a Nation Wept. It still is weeping. Theaters which closed bear no shame — no sign of weakness, but the love that every American must-have for their President.

In such a moment the walls — which I believe are necessary in holding our country, together — the walls which separate one political party from another come down. People from the north and south and east and west forget their political differences and weep the tears of suffering for their leader who is dead.

Why? — came the voice from Rome. Why? — came the voice from London England, Paris France, Bonn Germany, Moscow Russia, Ontario Canada, Sidney Australian, Tokyo Japan.

Why? Came the voices from every home in a nation that is still weeping. Why? There is but one answer: for the freedom of humankind. This is why Lincoln was assassinated — and Garfield and McKinley — and John F. Kennedy.

These men who served as our Presidents dedicated their lives to the freedom and dignity and respect that man should have and must have for one another. They did not die in vain unless we, who live on allow America to be destroyed and our Freedom taken from us.

And this goes much deeper than any animosity we have towards those countries we call our enemies. You do not preserve freedom through hate. You do not create freedom out of coercion.

The preservation of the world depends upon our accepting one another despite these differences or ideological thinking. It is this balance of power that has thus far preserved America — the wall of differences between one party and another.

In a very real sense, the death of our President should make us re-think our own part in the political structure of our nation. It should make us read and re-read American History until every stream, and avenue, is discovered anew. It should keep us abreast of this land, causing us to give something instead of always wanting something.

We moan of taxation — our minds are burdened with grievances and complaints; and yet did you ever stop, to think that this is a part of your freedom. Our blessings in this land are so great that all we have time for is to complain; we have no time to go down on our knees and thank God for America.

> 0 beautiful for spacious skies,
> For amber waves of grain,
> For purple mountain majesties,
> Above the fruited plain!
>
> And crown thy good with brotherhood
> From sea to shining sea.

The continuation and preservation of our land are no longer dependent upon the 35th President of the United States, who gave his life for that cause. It falls upon our 36th President, upon our willingness to work with him and pray for and love him. Symbolically speaking this is a new birth of freedom, which has arisen out of this tragic event.

Its survival will depend upon the wholeness of its creation: and its wholeness in turn depends upon God. Who in the first instant gave to us this new birth of freedom. Where then shall we go from here as Americans, as Christians?

There is only one place we can go — or one place from where we can start. We must start with prayer. First, a prayer of sorrow for our President who lost his life for this freedom. Second, a prayer for our new President.

> Jesus said to her, "Your brother will rise again."
>
> Martha said to him, "I know that he will rise again in the resurrection at the last day.
>
> "Jesus said to her, "I am the resurrection and the life; he who believes in me, though he dies, yet shall he live, and whoever lives and believes in me shall never die." Do you believe this? "…. Yes, Lord, I believe."
>
> And in a little while he said to her again; "Did I not tell you that if you would believe you would see the glory of God?"
>
> And he cried out with a loud voice, "Lazarus, come out."
>
> The dead man came out, his hands and feet bound with bandages, and his face wrapped with a cloth. Jesus said to them, "Unbind him, and let him go."

This is what Jesus is saying to our deceased President, to our New President — even to you and to me.

"Unbind him, and let him go!"

This is your new birth of freedom — to go now; go stripped of that which has bound you unto death —- go in His name and for His sake.

In closing might there be a moment of silent prayer. There may be those who would prefer to come and kneel at the rail here this morning. If you feel so compelled — do so. Come quickly and go quickly so that others may come too.

>Breathe on me, Breath of God,
>fill me with life anew,
>that I may love the way you love,
>and do what you would do.
>
>For all the saints who from labors rest,
>Who Thee by faith before the world confessed,
>Thy Name, O Jesus be forever blest.
>Alleluia, Alleluia!

Sermon delivered at Valley View Methodist Church in Overland Park, Kansas, on November 24, 1963.

SOMETHING MORE THAN PALMS

Palm Sunday — April 7, 1968

THREE DAYS AFTER the assassination of Martin Luther King Jr., a day declared by then–President Lyndon B. Johnson as a national day of mourning, for Christians it was Palm Sunday.

THERE IS NO ROOM for violence and destruction in this great country whether it be the rioting and violence of Black America or the subtle and poisonous mind of racial prejudice, which reaches out and cuts us from within, time after time, to destroy and dehumanize our civilization.

Jesus, —knowing he would meet death returned to Jerusalem. He wept bitterly over that city. He died for that city and the world, but his truth goes marching on.

Zechariah 9:9 – The Coming Ruler of God's People

> Rejoice greatly, O daughter of Zion!
>   Shout aloud, O daughter of Jerusalem!
> Lo, your king comes to you;
>   triumphant and victorious is he,
> humble and riding on an ass,
>   on a colt the foal of an ass.

Zechariah (9:9), the prophet, has spoken. In the year 530 B.C. he "began to prophesy," his was the period following the Jews return from exile. It was also the period of Jewish history when the people's hearts and minds were heavy and filled with hopelessness and discouragement; we catch something of this in the 5th chapter of Lamentations.

Lamentations 5:1 – A Plea for Mercy

"Remember, O Lord, what has befallen us;

behold, and see our disgrace!

Our inheritance has been turned over to strangers,

our homes to aliens."

Into this setting Zechariah came. Empathizing with the feelings of his people — reaching out to them, loving them — knowing of their discouragement and hopelessness, he gave them hope. He prophesied saying:

Zechariah 10:6 & 12 – Restoration of Judah and Israel

"I will strengthen the house of Judah,

and I will save the house of Joseph.

I will bring them back because I have compassion on them,

and they shall be as though I had not rejected them;

for I am the Lord their God and I will answer them.

12 I will make them strong in the Lord

and they shall glory in his name,"

says the Lord."

Zechariah has spoken...

Zechariah 9:9 – The Coming Ruler of God's People

"Rejoice greatly, O daughter of Zion!

Shout aloud, O Daughter of Jerusalem!

Lo, your king comes to yon

triumphant and victorious is he,

humble and riding on an ass,

on a colt the foal of an ass."

And some five hundred years later he did come. He marched triumphantly and victoriously into the city of Jerusalem.

He came riding an ass as Zechariah had prophesied.

"Spread on the ground before him, were garments, and branches of palm trees."

"Hosanna to the Son of David! Blessed is he who comes in the name of the Lord." — "Hosanna in the Highest!"

Use Our Imagination

We too can see Him —there. He is among the throng. A vast multitude has come out to — greet him. Some are waving.

Some are shouting. Some are there out of curiosity; I know of no greater description of this event than is found in Lloyd C. Douglas book, *The Robe*, for caught in the press of that crowd was the Greek slave Demetrius.

THE ROBE by Lloyd C. Douglas – Excerpts from Chapter V

"Standing on tiptoe for an instant in the swaying crowd, Demetrius caught a fleeting glimpse of the obvious centre of interest, a brown-haired, bareheaded, well–favoured Jew. A tight little circle had been left open for the slow advance of the shaggy white donkey on which he rode. It instantly occurred to Demetrius that this coronation project was an impromptu affair for which no preparation had been made.

Certainly, there were no efforts to bedeck the pretender with any royal regalia. He was clad in a simple brown mantle with no decorations of any kind, and the handful of men — his intimate friends, no doubt — who tried to shield him from the pressure of the throng wore the commonest sort of country garb.

Again Demetrius, regaining his lost balance, stretched to a full height for another look at the man who somehow evoked all this wild adulation. It was difficult to believe that this was the sort of person who could be expected to inflame a mob into some audacious action. Instead of receiving the applause with an air of triumph—or even of satisfaction — the unresponsive man on the white donkey seemed sad about the whole affair. He looked as if he would gladly have had none of it.

'Can you see him?' called the little Athenian, who had stuck fast in the sticky-hot pack an arm's length away.

Demetrius nodded without turning his head.

'Old man?'

In My Father's House Are Many Mansions

'No, not very,' answered Demetrius, candidly remote.

'What does he look like?' shouted the Athenian, impatiently.

Demetrius shook his head — and his hand, too — signaling that he couldn't be bothered now, especially with questions as hard to answer as this one.

'Look like a king?' yelled the little Greek, guffawing boisterously.

Demetrius did not reply. Tugging at his impounded garments, he crushed his way forward. The surging mass, pushing hard from the rear, now carried him on until he was borne almost into the very hub of the procession that edged along, step-by-step, keeping pace with the plodding donkey...

...Now there was a temporary blocking of the way, and the noisy procession came to a complete stop. The man on the white donkey straightened as if roused from a reverie, sighed deeply, and slowly turned his head. Demetrius watched, with parted lips and a pounding heart...

...Everyone was shouting, shouting — all but the Corinthian slave, whose throat was so dry he couldn't have shouted, who had no inclination to shout, who wished they would all be quiet, quiet! It wasn't the time or place for shouting. Quiet! This man wasn't the sort of person one shouted at or shouted for. Quiet! That was what this moment called for — Quiet!

Gradually, the brooding eyes moved over the crowd until they came to rest on the strained, bewildered face of Demetrius. The eyes calmly appraised Demetrius. They neither widened nor smiled; even so, in some indefinable manner, they held Demetrius in a grip so firm it was almost a physical compulsion. The message, they communicated, was something other than sympathy, something more vital than friendly concern; a sort of stabilizing power that swept away all such negations as slavery, poverty, or any other afflicting circumstance. Demetrius was suffused with the glow of this curious kinship. Blind with sudden tears, he elbowed through the throng and reached the roadside. The uncouth Athenian, bursting with curiosity, inopportunely accosted him.

'See him—close up?' he asked.

Demetrius nodded; and, turning away, began to retrace his steps toward his abandoned duty.

"Crazy?" persisted the Athenian, trudging alongside.

'No.'

'King?'

'No,' muttered Demetrius, soberly, 'not a king.'

'What is he, then?' demanded the Athenian, piqued by the Corinthian's aloofness.

'I don't know,' mumbled Demetrius, in a puzzled voice, 'but—he is something more important than a king.'"

Something more than a King…

There in the midst of the throng were all sorts of people. Let us see if we can identify them, the subject, and the object. Now we are standing in front of a mirror —the recollection of the crowd comes back to us. What do we see?

First, we see the curious ones. Not truly caring for the man Jesus, not knowing who it is that has attracted the crowd's attention, but simply present because of the throng. A crowd conforming once again, to the winds that swept across Jerusalem that day and in the days immediately ahead.

There is the blind man.

The woman caught in the act of adultery.

The crippled boy.

And, there, a young man who cannot hear…

Can we find ourselves in this crowd?

What infirm condition do we take with us? Are we there and are we here, this morning out of curiosity or have we come in search of a meaningful faith?

Second, there are those in the throng who have come once again to trap Jesus. Now they are more sure than ever they will reach their goal — accomplish their task.

Paying taxes to Caesar

Healing on the Sabbath

Stoning to death a woman who sinned.

She broke the commandment "Thou shalt not commit adultery."

And then there is Judas! Someone used him.

Politics — Using people.

Something More Than Palms

Third, and the most important person in the midst of the throng on that Palm Sunday was Jesus himself.

Something More Than A King.

Yes, — King of kings and Lord of lords.

He was the Saviour of the world. He had been sent by God to save the world, but the world knew him not. Only a few of his own people really understood this man Jesus. Only a few men today understand him and are willingly to give their lives for him, Jesus was 33 when he died.

He healed the sick. He caused the blind to see the lame to walk. Even so, such miracles as these did not kill Jesus. It was the political and economic and social changes, which he advocated that killed him. It was the same injustice, which he spoke against that finally put to him to death.

The hatred of men; not the love which he taught and exemplified brought him to that cross on Calvary.

The man, who was killed by an assassin's bullet last Thursday night, was killed because he too advocated political and economic and social justice for all men. I do not really want to talk about Martin Luther King, Jr. this morning. It Is Too Painful…

And yet, I must, even though I know you are exhausted of the subject, and I too, am exhausted. It was not my intention even to mention race and prejudice in today's sermon, and of the things I have prayed about since my coming to you, is that I would not alienate you or cause you to think that I was trying to coerce the love which God has given me for the black people on you.

I do not want to do either of these things this morning.
So, I'm going to stop preaching — right now!

I'm going to talk to you as you talk to me when there is a death in your family. I do not seek your respect for the man who meant so much to me; I only seek your love in sharing with me the pain and suffering which the event of history has thrust upon me in the tragic death and loss of my brother.

I talk out of deep pain, sorrow, grief. It was in 1963 that I first came to know Martin Luther King. I was fresh out of seminary and had struggled with some of the problems of life, including racial prejudice. However, I never took it seriously.

A part of my bringing up was to play it safe; don't be controversial. Don't get involved.

And then I received this letter from Martin Luther King, and I cried, and sometimes I still cry when I read it. This is where my brother has been misunderstood because people have seen only the violence, which often has followed the non-violent movement.

Martin Luther King, Jr. never carried a gun or a knife from the day he walked into the Baptist Church in Montgomery, Alabama, following his seminary and doctorate at Boston University. He preached love, and he died because of it. I wish there was time to read the whole letter but let me complete it by sharing the last few paragraphs.

A Letter from Birmingham Jail — A vigorous, eloquent reply to criticism expressed by a group of eight clergymen.

"Things are different now. So often the contemporary church is a weak, ineffectual voice with an uncertain sound. So often it is an arch defender of the status quo. Far from being disturbed by the presence of the church, the power structure of the average community is consoled by the church's silent — and often even vocal — sanction of things as they are.

Nevertheless, the judgment of God is upon the church as never before. If today's church does not recapture the sacrificial spirit of the early church, it will lose its authenticity, forfeit the loyalty of millions, and be dismissed as an irrelevant social club with no meaning for the 20th century. Every day I meet young people whose disappointment with the church has turned into outright disgust.

Perhaps — I have once again been too optimistic. Is organized religion too inextricably bound to the status quo to save our nation and the world? Perhaps — I must turn my faith to the inner spiritual church, the church within the church, as the true ecclesia and the hope of the world. But again, I am thankful to God that some noble souls from the ranks of organized religion have broken loose from the paralyzing chains of conformity and joined us as active partners in the struggle for freedom.

They have left their secure congregations and walked the streets of Albany, Georgia, with us. They have gone down the highways of the south on torturous rides for freedom. Yes, they have gone to jail with us. Some have been kicked out of their churches; have lost the support of their bishops and fellow ministers.

But they have acted in the faith that right defeated is stronger than evil triumphant. Their witness has been the spiritual salt that has preserved the true meaning of the gospel in these troubled times. They have carved a tunnel of hope through the dark mountain of disappointment."

Something More than Palms!

Jesus — knowing he would meet death — returned to Jerusalem. He wept bitterly over that city. He died for that city and the world, but his truth goes marching on.

There is no room for violence and destruction in this great country, whether it be the rioting and violence of Black America or the subtle and poisonous mind of prejudice, which reaches out and cuts us from within, time after time, to destroy and dehumanize our civilization.

I would pray that both groups might reorder their lives and rather than have a hell on earth, which is more than a possibility. We might strive to have one nation, under God, indivisible, with liberty and justice for all.

Let us pray!

Historical Note: In the aftermath of Martin Luther King Jr.'s assassination, there followed a nationwide wave of riots in more than 100 cities; this was the greatest wave of social unrest the United States had experienced since the Civil War. People were scared, White America was scared. This sermon was delivered in this social and racial context at St. Paul's United Methodist Church in Beaumont, Texas.

Two months later, on June 6, 1968, the nation witnessed the assassination of Robert F. Kennedy.

Sermon delivered at St. Paul's United Methodist Church in Beaumont, Texas on Sunday – April 7, 1968 – three days after the assassination of Martin Luther King Jr.

YOU'VE GOT TO BE CAREFULLY TAUGHT

To Hate and Fear – June 9, 1968 – After the death of Senator Robert Francis "Bobby" Kennedy

THOUGHTS by Edna K. Starbuck

They come in my mind at night mostly
when I want to rest or sleep
Or – just to be still.
They come sure as day.
Like footsteps in the dark.
Quiet and far away at first.
Then closer and heavier,
Almost staring, it seems,
Into – my mind's eye.
Not giving me any peace
Until I get up to let them out.
Then with pen and paper
I sit down and set them free.

THIS POEM written by my wife is an example of her poetic talent and her ability to engage with the deeper meaning of life. We have been married close to twenty years and through the years, there have been no expectations or strings attached. She has always set me free *(much more than I have set her free)* to do with my life what God intended me to do. And to be as creative as she is, with the thoughts which she puts down on paper, with the movements of her hand and the aid of a pen.

Such a gift of freedom comes only through one's absolute commitment to Jesus the Christ, who can set us free. As a youth stated at our Texas Annual Conference a few days ago: "Once we make this unconditional commitment we are 'set free' to love others no matter who they are or what they look like."

It is 5:57AM, Thursday morning, June 6th. I have just returned to my motel room with a cup of hot coffee and the tragic news of the death of Senator Robert F. Kennedy. The morning before I woke to find my radio and later television tell of his hospitalization following the blast of shots, which wounded five other people at the Ambassador Hotel in Los Angeles. I thought again of the lyrics of a Rodgers & Hammerstein song. A song I have quoted from on several occasions. The words seem so appropriate that I offer them to you and to your children and to mine — once again.

You've Got to Be Carefully Taught
South Pacific — Rodgers & Hammerstein

You've got to be taught to hate and fear,
You've got to be taught from year to year,
It's got to be drummed in your dear little ear
You've got to be carefully taught.

You've got to be taught to be afraid of people
Whose eyes are oddly made,
And people whose skin is a different shade,
You've got to be carefully taught.

You've got to be taught before it's too late
Before you are six or seven or eight,
To hate all the people your relatives hate
You've got to be carefully taught.

The same hatred for the Jewish people by Robert F. Kennedy's assassin is possessed by many people in this land, in this community, in churches for people of another race. Most of the time its possession is on an unconscious level but every so often something is said, or some action is taken and all that pus–flowing ugliness and hatred comes to the surface and filters the air with its fear, and poison, which intoxicates — the best of us.

A year ago, I stood in this pulpit a stranger in your midst. My sermon title was *You Are Accepted*. As I talked about your acceptance and mine and how it comes about through God's grace, I shared the following words of theologian Paul Tillich with you.

"In the light of this grace we perceive the power of in our relation to others and to ourselves. We experience the grace of being able to look frankly into the eyes of another, the miraculous grace of reunion of life with life. We experience the grace of understanding each other's words. We understand not merely the literal meaning of the words, but also, even when they are harsh or angry. For even then there is a longing to break through the walls of separation.

We experience the grace of being able to accept the life of another, even if it be hostile and harmful to us, for, through grace, we know that it belongs to the same Ground (the same God) to which we belong and by which we have been accepted. We experience the grace which is able to overcome the tragic separation of the sexes, of the generations, of the nations, of the races, and even the utter strangeness between man and nature. Sometimes grace appears in all these separations to reunite us with those to whom we belong. For life belongs to life." – Paul Tillich

Do you remember the death of Dr. Tom Dooley, the great American Missionary in Laos?

In his book *The Night They Burned the Mountain* he tells of the personal, battle he fought against cancer while healing the sick in the jungles of Asia.

At first, Tom Dooley was unwilling to be accepted by his Creator even though he ministered to the people of Laos in order to set them free. His unwillingness in this instance in not accepting his Creator was his unwillingness to face the reality of his disease. Still, such acceptance was to come to this great person, and he was to write;

"From my hospital bed in New York with the same white light of revelation I had known once several years before, I saw what I must do. After Communion that morning, Tuesday, the first of September, my God, and my dream commanded me.

I must, into the burnt soil of my personal mountain of sadness. plant the new seedlings of my life — I must continue to live. I must cultivate my fields of food, to feed those who cannot feed themselves.

The concept came to me as strongly and as powerfully as if a peal of bronze bells proclaimed it. There was no more self-sadness, no darkness deep inside; no gritty annoyance at anyone or anything. No anger at God for my cancer, no hostility to anyone. I was out of the fog of confusion standing under the clear light of duty. The jagged, ugly cancer scar went no deeper than my flesh. There was no cancer in my spirit. The Lord saw to that. I would keep my appetite for fruitful activity and for a high quality of life.

Whatever time was left, whether it was year or a decade, would be more than just a duration. I would continue to help the clots and clusters of withered and wretched in Asia to the utmost of my ability. The words of Camus rang through, "In the midst of winter I suddenly found that there was in me an invincible summer.""

You are accepted! No strings attached. In giving your life to God you are set free. As the children of Tom Dooley's favorite Texan family wrote him from Ft. Worth having composed new words to the tune "Hang Down Your Head, Tom Dooley."

Lift up your heart, Tom Dooley,
Your work will never die.
You taught us to love our neighbor
And not just to pass him by.

We'll pray for you, Tom Dooley,
Your cure and your patients, too.
We'll send in our dimes and dollars

For work that's left to do

Lift up your head, Tom Dooley,
Life up your head, don't cry.
Lift up your head, Tom Dooley,
Cause you ain't a-goin to die.

Even though his physical life was taken Tom Dooley never died, neither did John Kennedy nor Martin Luther King nor Robert Kennedy nor all the others who have given themselves for freedom's sake. So much bigger than you and me, so far ahead of us in our thinking than we can and must but follow them. No strings attached.

It is a new day shared by all faiths and all denominations, by all who will participate in it and not be afraid of losing their own life. For if they lose it for His sake, they shall find it.

This was my first annual conference of Methodism in the state of Texas. I must say I was deeply impressed by the growth and creativity that went on in Houston this past week.

As the Pharisees would have denied the woman to have communion with Jesus, so we often refuse those who we consider less righteous than ourselves, a fellowship in the Church of Jesus Christ.

"Then he turned to the woman and said to Simon; do you see this woman? I came into your home and you gave me no water for my feet, but she has washed my feet with her tears and dried them with her hair. You did not welcome me with a kiss, but she has not topped kissing my feet since I came. You provided no oil for my head, but she has covered my feet with perfume. I tell you, then the great love she has shown proves that her many sins have been forgiven."

I have a dream that we too shall be forgiven for all of our sins, with no strings attached. That is, only the string of love that we might love others. I have a dream that the good in this church, in this nation, in this world will overcome the evil be it the violence of an assassin's bullet or the verbal expression of utter hate and hostility.

No wonder one great martyr was able to write, "I have a dream that one day every valley shall be exalted, every hill and mountain shall be made low. The rough places will be made plain, and the crooked places will be made straight. With this faith we will be able to hew out of the mountains of despair a stone of hope. With this faith we will be able to work together, to pray together, to struggle together....This will be the day when all of God's children will be able to sing with new meaning, 'let freedom ring.'

So, let freedom ring from the prodigious hilltops of Hew Hampshire. Let freedom ring from the mighty mountains of New York. But not only that. Let freedom ring from Stone Mountain of Georgia. Let freedom ring from every hill and molehill of Mississippi, from every mountain side, then we allow freedom to ring when we let it ring from every city and every hamlet, from every state and every city, we will be able to speed up that day when all of God's children, black men and white men, Jews and Gentiles, Protestants and Catholics, will be able to join hands and sing in the words of the old Negro spiritual, 'Free at last, Free at last, Great God a-mighty, We are free at last."

— Martin Luther King Jr. *I Have a Dream*

Amen

Sermon delivered at St. Paul's United Methodist Church in Beaumont, Texas on June 9, 1968 – three days after the death of Senator Robert Francis Kennedy.

SOMETHING MORE IMPORTANT

Than dividing a church or a nation into conservatives and liberals.

AND BEHOLD, there was a man with a withered hand. And they asked him, "Is it lawful to heal on the Sabbath?" so they might accuse him. He said to them, "What man of you, if he has one sheep and it falls into a pit on the Sabbath, will not lay hold of it and lift it out? Of how much more value is a man than a sheep! So, it is lawful to do good on the Sabbath." Then he said to the man, "Stretch out your hand," And the man stretched it out and it was restored, whole like the other. But the Pharisees went out and took counsel against him, how to destroy him. ~ Matthew 12:10-14

SOMETHING MORE IMPORTANT! On Sunday morning, June 28th, I woke up to the sounds of birds singing in the trees; the brightness of the morning sun already found its way across the foot of my bed. It was a restful night — no fans, no Air-condition; only the cool breeze of a summer night 800 miles north of Houston. I woke knowing this was to be a very special day.

There was still hay in the field that had been cut the day before. It needed to be baled and put into the barn. We were at Edna's folks, and I'm sure her father of 75 years thought about the hay that morning and in his own way — wished that it was all baled and stored safely away for the winter. Even so, if the thought ever passed his mind, it was soon forgotten that day —because something more important was about to happen. On the day's agenda was a forthcoming celebration; fifty years of married life.

Edna's brother and wife arrived at the farm shortly after 7:30 a.m. All of us were in the process of dressing for Morning Worship. Church service began at 8:30. By the time everyone was ready (which was about 8:15) Edna's dad was pacing the floor. I was helping him. He was not used to waiting, I could tell he was impatient, but he didn't say anything. After all, this was a special day —something' more important.

Soon we were in the cars, —driving north over a hill or two until we reached one of the main arteries running east and west. We turned right, and half a mile took us to St. John Lutheran Church where Edna, and I were married; and where Dad and Mom Meinert were united in a service of holy matrimony one–half century ago. As a large family, we took up one whole pew. Everyone knew why we were there because in every small rural setting, everyone knows about everyone else. The celebration of worship seemed so appropriate in setting the climate for the day ahead.

Young and old, rich, and poor relatives and friends gathered that afternoon in the parish hall across the road. They came to celebrate — to offer congratulations and add their blessings. The best man and the maid of honor — the two people who stood up with them 50 years ago were present. The fields were silent that afternoon; untouched by man or machinery. There was something more important taking place.

It is wonderful that every now and then we can stop moving in this busy world of ours and join with others in a great event or celebration.

It reminds us that we too are but mortal creatures and while we belong to the infinite, we are still finite in nature. Sometimes death interrupts our lives —the death of someone we love. Sometimes sickness interrupts our lives or an emergency operation or a routine tonsillectomy.

The other night I scheduled two appointments and a meeting at 8 O'clock. At approximately 5:40 PM, the telephone rang; our oldest daughter needed help. She was running a high fever; complications from her tonsillectomy of two weeks ago. We discovered later that she had a severe inner ear infection. I had to cancel my appointment because of something more important.

Take the story of one of the senior pastors in a large Methodist Church in Houston; I was talking to him only last Monday. He was sharing some of his problems with three other ministers, including myself. A letter went out from his study at the end of May asking his people to continue their church pledge through December of this year. The Conference decided to go on a fiscal year beginning January 1st. If you recall, I talked about this last fall, so we got the jump on a lot of other churches, the wisdom of a fool.

He went ahead to tell us that he received a letter from one layperson canceling his pledge because the church was too liberal. The very next day he received a letter from another layperson canceling his pledge because the church was too conservative. In a moment of deep frustration, he cried out, "What am I to do!" The question may seem trivial to you but to this pastor, it was very important. It concerned him ultimately; "What am I to do?"

I wished that I could have given him the answer, but I don't have the answer. Oh, I have an answer but not, the answer. My answer would be to him and to you and to myself that there is something more important.

There is something more important than dividing a church or a nation into conservatives and liberals. The two words have really come to bother me for I think they are over used, and we are obsessed with them. I do not think that a Christian can be one or the other. He must be both. We must conserve and liberate at the same time. We can never sever our ties from that part of history, which belongs to us.

The teachings of the Bible —the rule and guide of faith —our faith, is just as relevant now as it was two thousand years ago. Just because we live in a new day and must continually interpret the importance of God's word for our day does not mean that we throw the baby out with the bath water. You simply do not cut off the past to get to the problems of the future or even to the problems of this day — here and now.

There is a danger in a closed mind. We must always look in both directions. Therefore, we conserve and liberate at the same time.

Something More Important! Jesus was both conservative and liberal. He was open to the future, but he did not destroy the past. He came not to destroy the law and the prophets but to fulfill them.

Again, and again, he referred to the teachings as found in the law and the prophets. They served as the very basis of his sermon —even his Sermon on the Mount. And yet at the same time he offered something new.

"A new commandment I give you; that you love one another even as I have loved you."

You have heard that it was said of old, but I say of you...

Jesus conserved and liberated at the same time. He did not destroy the past, but he always moved out in such a way as to give life to others and to set them free.

Something More Important! Let us enlarge our Text this morning and examine the contents, which appears in the early part of the 12th chapter of Matthew, the Pharisees, caught up in their own way of life were threatened by Jesus.

They were very legalistic in their interpretation of the Law and the Prophets. Jesus was adding a new light to that interpretation. They did not know how to cope with this Jesus, so they moved out to destroy him. Eventually they were successful. They caught their game. Humanity can be successful in destroying other human beings; but it is something else to be so free, and at peace with yourself that you can give this same feeling of freedom and peace to others.

Something More Important! Speaking to the parents and members of a graduating class of Pasadena Independent School District a week ago Friday night, I asked them to imagine that they were at a Rock Festival or in a high school auditorium or sitting in a chair viewing their television. I then asked them to listen to the following words as sung by a Rock group known as **Traffic**.

"Crying' to Be Heard" — Written by Dave Mason

Traffic – Studio Album Released October 1968 — "Cryin' To Be Heard" – – Recorded Olympic Studios, London, Record Plant, NYC, January–May 1968

Mason – lead vocal; Winwood – bass, Hammond – organ, harpsichord, backing vocal; Wood – soprano saxophone; Capaldi – drums, backing vocal.

    Somebody's cryin' to be heard
    And there's also someone who hears every word

    Sail across the ocean with your back against the wind
    Listening to nothing save the calling of a bird
    And when the rain begins to fall, don't you start to curse
    It may be just the tears of someone that you never heard

    Somebody's cryin' to be heard
    And there's also someone who hears every word

    Reflected in the water is a face that you don't know
    And isn't it surprising when you findin' out it's your own?
    And so, you try to find out whether it is friend or foe
    And what it is it wants from you and what it wants to know?

    Somebody's cryin' to be heard
    And there's also someone who hears every word

    Well, you're wrapped up in your little world and no one can get in
    You sit and think of everything then, then you wonder where you've been

You put the blame on someone that you've hardly ever known
And then you realize too late the blame was all your own

Somebody's cryin' to be heard
And there's also someone who hears every word

Sail across the ocean with your back against the wind
Listening to nothing save the calling of a bird
And when the rain begins to fall, don't you start to curse
It may be just the tears of someone that you never heard

Somebody's cryin' to be heard
And there's also someone who hears every word

Songwriter ~ MASON, DAVE

Something more important, than blaming others —than dividing a church or a nation into conservatives or liberals. Something more important; A new commandment I give you, that you love one another even as I have loved you.

Sermon delivered at Asbury United Methodist Church, Pasadena, Texas on August 9, 1970.

DO YOU SEE WHAT I SEE?
A Christmas Sermon

"DO YOU HEAR WHAT I HEAR?"
Lyrics by Noël Regney & Music by Gloria Shayne Baker

Said the night wind to the little lamb,
Do you see what I see?
Way up in the sky, little lamb,
Do you see what I see?
A star, a star, dancing in the night
With a tail as big as a kite,
With a tail as big as a kite.

Said the little lamb to the shepherd boy,
Do you hear what I hear?
Ringing through the sky, shepherd boy,
Do you hear what I hear?
A song, a song high above the trees
With a voice as big as the sea,
With a voice as big as the sea.

Said the shepherd boy to the mighty king,
Do you know what I know?
In your palace warm, mighty king,
Do you know what I know?
A Child, a Child shivers in the cold-
Let us bring him silver and gold,
Let us bring him silver and gold.

Said the king to the people everywhere,
Listen to what I say!
Pray for peace, people, everywhere,
Listen to what I say!

> The Child, the Child sleeping in the night
> He will bring us goodness and light,
> He will bring us goodness and light.

"DO YOU HEAR WHAT I HEAR?" is a carol first written in October 1962, with lyrics by Noël Regney and music by Gloria Shayne Baker; they were married at the time. The song was written as a plea for peace during the Cuban Missile Crisis; it has become one of the world's favorite Christmas carols.

IT IS STILL an important message to share. Especially, in a war-weary-world where it is long past time to end the religious strife that divides humankind so often. To come to some understanding of our common humanity, one that takes us beyond the tenets of any faith, in an interfaith dialogue and acceptance, as surely as Jesus taught us to love one another.

> It will soon be Christmas Eve and then Christmas morning!
>
> Do you hear what I hear? Do you hear the song high above the trees?
>
> Do you see what I see? Do you see the star dancing in the night?
>
> Do you know the child shivering in the cold?
>
> Listen to what I say: He has brought us goodness and light.

Thus, for Christians, begins the first day of Christmas. There will be twelve entire days before we arrive in Bethlehem to offer our gifts of gold and frankincense and myrrh, which will take place on January 6, another Christian feast day called Epiphany.

Epiphany means to manifest, to see a spiritual event unfold. This is a manifestation of the Divine love in human form, for Christians it is a celebration of the revelation of God as a human being in Jesus Christ. God's love made manifest in the world. And brings about an indwelling of the Spirit for all humankind.

This was and still is God's gift to us. We decorate our trees, our houses, our yards, and we become excited as we wait for the event to unfold. We even give gifts to others, which are symbolic of God's gift to us.

I work with children and even adults who know nothing about this gift. Christmas is simply a secular holiday in which school gets out for two weeks, and gifts are exchanged. They know there is a baby somewhere in the picture - Baby Jesus, they say, but other than the name, they know nothing about him. They don't know that he came to save the world from our sins - to make us whole again.

Do you know that people sing Amazing Grace - a catchy little tune, but have no real concept of what it is all about? It is sad because they are not even aware when Grace strikes them.

I cherish the words of Paul Tillich, noted theologian in his sermon "You Are Accepted," from his book *The Shaking of the Foundations*.

He says: "It would be better to refuse God and Christ and the Bible than to accept them without grace. For if we accept them without grace, we do so in the state of separation, and can only succeed in deepening the separation. We cannot transform our lives, unless we allow them to be transformed by that stroke of grace."

He goes ahead to say: "It happens, or it does not happen. And certainly, it does not happen if we try to force it upon ourselves, just as it shall not happen so long as we think, in our self-complacency, that we have no need of it. Grace strikes us when we are in great pain and restlessness.

It strikes us when we walk through the dark valley of a meaningless and empty life. It strikes us when we feel that our separation is deeper than usual, because we have violated another life, a life, which we loved, or from which we were estranged. It strikes us when our disgust for our own being, our indifference, our weakness, our hostility, and our lack of direction and composure has become intolerable to us.

It strikes us when, year after year, the longed-for perfection of life does not appear, when the old compulsions reign within us as they have for decades, when despair destroys all joy and courage. Sometimes at that moment a wave of light breaks into our darkness, and it is as though a voice were saying: You are accepted. You are accepted, accepted by that which is greater than you."

Love came down at Christmas. It can happen at Christmas, but it can happen at any time. After such an experience (a happening) we may not be better than before, and we may not believe more than before. But everything is transformed. In that moment grace conquers sin, and reconciliation bridges the gulf of estrangement. And nothing is demanded of this experience, no religious or moral or intellectual presuppositions, nothing but acceptance.

I think now of Jeremiah, known as the Prophet of Prayer. "This is the covenant I will make with them I will put my law within them, and I will write it upon their hearts; and I will be their God, and they shall be my people." Jeremiah made God very personal for he told the people that they shall, all know me from the least of them to the greatest.

Then John in the New Testament tells the story of Nicodemus. "Truly, truly, I say to you, unless one is born anew, he cannot see the kingdom of God." Nicodemus did not understand Jesus' saying.

He asked, "How can a man be born when he is old?" We now know that being born of the spirit has nothing to do with chronological age. It has nothing to do with one's social or economic status. It does have something to do about being struck by grace.

Christmas is certainly about such grace — about being transformed. Once this happens we know what it is to be one of his disciples. We know something about discipleship - knowing what it is all about and living it. The poet Ann Weems has provided us with a beautiful poem in her book *Kneeling in Bethlehem*. I used it five or six years ago.

CHRISTMAS TREES AND STRAWBERRY SUMMERS
by Ann Weems

What I'd really like is a life of Christmas trees and
strawberry summers,
A walk through the zoo with a pocketful of bubble gum and
    a string of balloons.
I'd say "yes" to blueberry mornings and carefree days
    with rainbow endings,
I'd keep the world in springtime and the morning glories
    blooming.
But life is more than birthday parties;
    life is more than candied apples.

I'd rather hear the singing than the weeping.
I'd rather see the healing than the violence.
I'd rather feel the pleasure than the pain.
I'd rather know security than fear.
I'd like to keep the cotton candy coming,
but life is more than fingers crossed;
    life is more than wishing.

Christ said, "follow me."
And, of course, I'd rather not.
I'd rather pretend that doesn't include me.
I'd rather sit by the fire and make my excuses.
I'd rather look the other way,
    not answer the phone,
    and be much too busy to read the paper.

But I said yes and
    that means risk—

it means, here I am, ready or not!

O Christmas trees and strawberry summers,
you're what I like, and you are real.
But so are hunger
      and misery
      and hate-filled red faces.
So is confrontation.
So is injustice.
Discipleship means sometimes it's going to rain in my face.

But when you've been blind and now you see,
      when you've been deaf and now you hear,
      when you've never understood and now you
know,
      once you know who God calls you to be,
      you're not content with sitting in corners.
There's got to be some alleluia shouting,
      some speaking out
      some standing up
      some caring
      some sharing
      some community
      some risk.
Discipleship means living what you know.
Discipleship means "Thank you, Lord"
      for Christmas trees and strawberry summers
      and even for rain in my face.

Amen.

Sermon delivered at Sunset United Methodist Church in December 2008.

THE AFTERGLOW
A Christmastide Sermon

IMAGINE FOR A MOMENT that you are sitting in front of a campfire with the flame going up and down, back, and forth. You are mesmerized! You go on a journey to Never Neverland. You have no concept of time for 30 minutes or an hour is in itself lost in time.

Whoever was there a few minutes ago has left. You are all alone - quietness grips you and your thoughts return to the evening just ended and the future that awaits you. The fire before you is gone - only the burning embers remain - the afterglow.

It is the second Sunday in Christmastide. The decorations have already been taken down. The Christmas tree is gone, and the beautiful poinsettias too, but look! - We still have the cross, lectern, the pulpit, and the candles on the altar are still burning. We need to keep them burning for Christmas is not over. The Wise Men have not arrived. The Star in the East is still shining as they make their way to Bethlehem.

A couple of weeks ago, I was talking to the mother of our next-door neighbor. She was telling me with a sparkle in her eyes that her son, and his wife were in the process of adopting their second child. He would be arriving on January 6th.

I said, "O, that's a special day."

"That's your birthday?" she asked.

"No, that is Epiphany-the day the wise men arrived in Bethlehem with their gifts of Gold, Frankincense, and Myrrh."

Then I told her the story of the Twelve Days of Christmas. While she knew the song, she did not know the story. She is active in her church, but it doesn't follow the Christian year as we do.

Like the wise men, we too journey toward Bethlehem. We too want, even need to lay our gifts before the Lord Jesus. He's waiting for us – you know.

"Come to me, all who labour and are heavy laden, and I will give you rest. Take my yoke upon you, and learn from me, for I am gentle and lowly in heart, and you will find rest for your souls. For my yoke is easy, and my burden is light."

"You are the light of the world. A city set on a hill cannot be hid. Nor do men light a lamp and put it under a bushel, but on a stand, and it gives light to all in the house. Let your light so shine before men, that they may see your good works, and give glory to your Father who is in heaven."

Jesus admonishes us to love God but also to love one another and certainly love ourselves. I think now of the hundreds of people I have worked with through the years that do not love themselves. Since early childhood, they have been physically, emotionally, verbally, and many sexually abused. They depend on others to make them feel good – even to feel loved.

We are on this good earth to love and be loved. Listen to Luke as he writes: "And he came to Nazareth, where he had been brought up; and he went to the synagogue, as his custom was, on the Sabbath day. And he stood up to read, and there was given to him the book of the prophet Isaiah.

He opened the book and found the place where it was written, "The Spirit of the Lord is upon me, because he has anointed me to preach good news to the poor. He has sent me to proclaim release to the captives and recovering of sight to the blind, to set at liberty those who are oppressed."

The Prophet Jeremiah was often referred to as the suffering or weeping prophet; he prophesied in both the pre and post-exilic era. The Northern Kingdom had already fallen to the Assyrians and in 586 BC the Babylonians conquered the Southern Kingdom, and many were taken to Babylon. It was during their captivity that Jeremiah told them of the New Covenant God would make with the house of Israel and the house of Judah.

"I will put my law within them, and I will write it upon their hearts; and I will be their God, and they shall be my people. And no longer shall each man teach his neighbor and each his brother, saying, 'Know the Lord,' for they shall all know me, from the least of them to the greatest, says the Lord; for I will forgive their iniquity, and I will remember their sin no more."

During my years as a parish minister, I simply could not understand and later felt anger because certain church people were complaining that I was spending too much time with the youth. In the late 60s and early 70s, I loved going to Lakeview to work with the youth. I always enjoyed Youth Activity Week, which was so evident in churches throughout our Conference during that period of history. It reminds me of these two poems.

THE BUILDER
By Ms. Will Allen Dromgoole

An old man going a lone highway,
Came, at the evening cold and gray,
To a chasm vast and deep and wide.
Through which was flowing a sullen tide
The old man crossed in the twilight dim,
The sullen stream had no fear for him;
But he turned when safe on the other side
And built a bridge to span the tide.

"Old man," said a fellow pilgrim near,
"You are wasting your strength with building here;
Your journey will end with the ending day,

You never again will pass this way;
You've crossed the chasm, deep and wide,
Why build this bridge at evening tide?"

The builder lifted his old gray head;
"Good friend, in the path I have come," he said,
"There followed after me to-day
A youth whose feet must pass this way.
This chasm that has been as naught to me
To that fair-haired youth may a pitfall be;
He, too, must cross in the twilight dim;
Good friend, I am building this bridge for him!"

VOYAGERS
By Ruth Comfort Mitchell

A tired old doctor died today, and a baby boy was born–
A little new soul that was pink and frail, and a soul that was gray and worn.
And—halfway here and halfway there–
On a white, high hill of shining air,
They met and passed and paused to speak in the flushed and hearty dawn.

The man looked down at the soft, small thing, with wise and weary eyes;
And the little chap stared back at him, with startled, scared surmise:
And then he shook his downy head-
"I think I won't be born," he said;
"You are too gray and sad!" And he shrank from the pathway down the skies.

But the tired old doctor roused once more at the battle-cry of birth,
And there was memory in his look, of grief and toil and mirth,
"Go on!" he said, "It's good-and bad:
It's hard! Go on! It's ours, my lad."
And he stood and urged him out of sight, down to the waiting earth.

As we celebrate the afterglow of Christmas and wait for the wise men to arrive with their gifts may we gather up our own gifts – and continue on our journey with a life full of wonder and excitement. We too have seen his Star in the East and have come to worship him.

"I have come that you might have life and have it more abundantly."

"I am the Alpha and Omega, the Beginning, and the End. I am the Way, the Truth, and the Life."

It is the eighth day of Christmas. It is Epiphany Sunday. A new year awaits us. Our world awaits us.

Sermon delivered at Sunset United Methodist Church in January 2009.

THE QUEST BELONGS TO EACH OF US

We All Belong To God

"HE COMES TO US AS ONE UNKNOWN without a name, as of old, by the lake-side, He came to those who knew Him not. He speaks to us the same word: 'Follow thou Me!' and sets us to the task which he has to fulfill for our time. He commands. And to those who obey Him, whether they be wise or simple, He will reveal Himself in the toils, the conflicts, the sufferings which they shall pass through in His fellowship, and, as an ineffable mystery, they shall learn in their own experience who He is."

THESE MEMORABLE WORDS by Albert Schweitzer describe his *Quest of the Historical Jesus*, the title of his book, which was published in 1906. Schweitzer came from a family which for generations was devoted to religion, music, and education. His father and maternal grandfather were ministers, and both of his grandfathers were talented organists. Schweitzer himself became an accomplished organist, and at the age of nine performed in his father's church. At the age of 30, he chose to become a missionary in Africa rather than be a pastor of a local church. It was at this time that he began his studies in medicine, and later founded the hospital in Lambarene, Africa. He lived a full life and died at the age of 90.

Some say that he gave up the quest. I don't think so. I think in a given moment of time he was simply able to accept and acknowledge that each of us learns through our own experience who Jesus Christ is.

It happens, or it does not happen — God's grace. I preached on this the last Sunday in December. Once we experience God's grace then we're on our way. It reminds me of Bert Lancaster in the movie, *Elmer Gantry*. He has just jumped off a freight train and hears music coming from a small black church. He soon picks up the beat as he enters the church.

"I'm on my way. I'm on my way to Canaan land. I'm on my way, Gloria, Gloria. Alleluia."

Are you on your way? What is your quest? The quest belongs to each of us. We each walk a different road. We all belong to the same Being. God said to Moses, "I am who I am." And he said, "Say this to the people of Israel, I am has sent me to you." Was that the beginning of his search, his quest? Perhaps! The beginning for you and for me will find a different starting point.

The little girl had lost her grandfather. Picture in your mind this little girl. Listen carefully: "I ran, searching, searching. Grandfather, Where are you?" She stopped for a moment - resting against a wall, the warm tears rolling down her swollen cheek. Where have you gone? "Inside your heart, my love, a soft voice said - Inside!"

Was that the beginning of her quest? Be still and know that I am God. Jesus loves me yes; I know for the Bible tells me so. What did those words mean to you as a little child?

Accept it, enter into it, and let it grasp you. Those are the areas I will be focusing on this morning. If you bear with me and don't tell anyone you will find this sermon has three parts – three points for you to remember and take with you. Accept it, enter into it, and let it grasp you!

First, accept God's love. Don't ask any questions when you are struck by grace. Just for a moment let's look at Isaiah's call.

"In the year that King Uzziah died, I saw the Lord sitting upon a throne, high and lifted up, and his train filled the temple. Above him stood the seraphim; each had six wings; with two he covered his face, and with two he covered his feet, and with two he flew. And one called to another and said: "Holy, holy, holy is the Lord of hosts; the whole earth is full of his glory." And the foundations of the thresholds shook at the voice of him who called, and the house was filled with smoke. And I said, "Woe is me! For I am lost, for I am a man of unclean lips, and I dwell in the midst of a people of unclean lips; for my eyes have seen the King, the Lord of hosts."

Isaiah was spellbound – blinded. The unheard of — had happened, for with his own eyes he had seen Yahweh, the King, the Lord of hosts.

Immediately it brings to mind Paul's experience on the Road to Damascus: Now as he journeyed he approached Damascus, and suddenly a light from heaven flashed about him. And he fell to the ground and heard a voice saying to him, "Saul, Saul, why do you persecute me? " And he said, "Who are you Lord?" And he said, "I am Jesus, whom you are persecuting; but rise and enter the city, and you will be told what to do. " The men who were traveling with him stood speechless, hearing the voice but seeing no one. Saul arose from the ground; and when his eyes opened, he could see nothing; so, they led him by the hand and brought him into Damascus.

You know the rest of the story - after three days the Lord summoned Ananias who was called upon to heal Saul, who afterwards took the name of Paul for he was filled with the Holy Spirit, and his sight was restored.

We don't all experience such a dramatic moment as Paul and Isaiah encountered, but once we accept God's grace we are transformed – the old is gone, finished. A new creation has occurred. A new being has appeared, and as we accept it we find ourselves entering into it.

As one enters into it (the second point in this sermon) one takes upon himself or herself a mission. When Almondine in David Wroblewski's novel, *The Story of Edgar Sawtelle*, first heard the sound from Edgar's lips, she became spellbound. Almondine was a dog, and Edgar was the little boy born dumb. He could hear, but he could not speak.

When he made a gurgling sound, it could not be heard by the human ears, but it could be heard by the very sensitive ears of Almondine. Once Almondine understood this she took on the role of caring for, protecting, and shadowing Edgar. Almondine, not only accepted Edgar's muteness, but she entered into his very being. It is such a beautiful story, and if you have not read it put it on your list as a must.

As we read from the Good Book this morning, Jesus was on his way back from Judea to Galilee, and he had to pass through Samaria. It was on this journey that he met the woman at the well. She was astounded that this Jew could ask her, a woman of Samaria, for a drink of water.

As the story unfolds Jesus tells her of water, which is like a spring of water. Once a person drinks of this water, he shall never thirst. His cup shall always be full and over flowing for in the very realness of life, it is God's love. Once you enter into it, your life becomes a fountain, and the water (God's love) is not yours to keep but yours to share with every person you touch as you journey through life.

Once you have experienced God's love you are suddenly grasped by a power greater than you. So, we come to the last point in this sermon, for to be grasped by God means that you have been seized by His love. Is that the end or really the beginning of one's quest? Accept it, enter into it – let it grasp you!

"Amazing Grace how sweet the sound that saved a wretch

like me. I once was lost but now am found; was blind but

now I see."

The quest belongs to each of us. We never stop searching. The more we know about the historical Jesus, the more we realize that such knowledge is too wonderful. It is too high for these finite minds to attain, and it isn't until we let go that the Jesus of History becomes for us the Christ of Faith. We're in the very midst of the Lenten Season. This is the third Sunday in Lent. Three more Sundays takes us to Palm Sunday, the beginning of Holy Week. The quest continues, and the drama of your faith and my faith unfolds before our very eyes.

A young woman was in my office a few weeks ago. I took her through a relaxation exercise and after awakening her from her trance, I asked her how she felt. She seemed almost embarrassed with tears softly rolling down her cheek. She quietly told me that suddenly, she felt loved by God. There was no reason for her to feel that way. I never made any hypnotic suggestion that would have triggered such a thought or feeling. She simply was struck by grace. Accept it, enter in to it, let it grasp you!

"He comes to us as one Unknown without a name, as of old, by the lake-side, He came to those who knew Him not. He speaks to us the same word: 'Follow thou Me!' and sets us to the task which he has to fulfill for our time. He commands. And to those who obey Him, whether they be wise or simple, He will reveal Himself in the toils, the conflicts, the sufferings which they shall pass through in His fellowship, and, as an ineffable mystery, they shall learn in their own experience who He is."

Amen.

Pastoral Prayer

We continue our journey, Lord, for it is the Lenten Season. We walk with you to the Cross for this is a time of preparation. I wonder what it was really like — the last six weeks of your Son's life. It seems at times that even he couldn't understand what you had in store for him. At one point, he felt forsaken by you. There was an inner struggle going on for he didn't want to die. He finally cried out: "Not my will but let your will be done." So here we are, Lord, each one of us struggling to be free. Help us to feel your love so we in turn can love others. We pray for our brothers and sisters everywhere; and I suppose selfishly in a way we lift up those persons whose names were read because so many of them are known by so many of us. Let thy healing power, touch each person in a special way. Allow us to join hands that our love will be felt throughout all who gather here this morning. In Jesus's name, we pray. Amen.

Sermon delivered at Sunset United Methodist Church in March 2009.

TO LIVE IS TO LOVE
The Acceptance of Belonging

TO LIVE IS TO LOVE. In God's love we live and move and have our being for God is love; and if we believe in the name of his son Jesus Christ and love one another, just as he has commanded us, so we abide in him and he in us. The one cannot be separated from the other anymore than a branch can be separated from the vine. "I am the vine you are the branches. He who abides in me, and I in him, he it is that bears much fruit, for apart from me you can do nothing."

To live is to love. The one cannot be separated from the other anymore than a branch can be separated from the vine. As we examine this theme, may we do so in part with the personage of Socrates in mind, namely, that the unexamined life is not worth living. Let us also do so with these three thoughts in mind: (1) The consciousness of things, (2) The acceptance of belonging, and (3) The reunion of the separation.

The consciousness of things. Our knowledge of the world, our knowledge of things within the world are not known by us until we become conscious of the world. So, it is with God. The knowledge of God, the very existence of God becomes known to us only as we become conscious of His presence here and now. The prophetic voice of God, His way and His truth and His life become a part of you only as you become conscious and aware of Him.

The knowledge of things are made known to us when we become aware of them; but the things themselves take on life only as we see them through the eyes of the Eternal. This is what Friedrich Schleiermacher was saying in his essay *On Religion*.

In the following words Schleiermacher describes the religious person and how such a person sees the universal existence of all finite things in and through the Infinite.

"Religion is to seek this and find it in all that lives and moves, in all growth and change, in all doing and suffering. It is to have life and to know life in immediate feeling, only as such an existence in the Infinite and Eternal. Where this is found religion is satisfied, where it hides itself there is for her unrest and anguish, extremity, and death. Wherefore it is a life in the infinite nature of the Whole, in the One and in the All, in God, having and possessing all things in God, and God in all."

> To live is to love. To live is to be of God and in God,
> for God is love.

Beyond the consciousness of things is the acceptance of belonging. As a creature living on this earth, you belong to Him who created you – God. Unless there is an acceptance of belonging on your part then there is actually no belonging. You may be in a state of physical existence, but unless there is the acceptance of belonging to Him who is Life, then there is no life. You belong to God, as surely as you belong to this world. But unless you accept this fact within your own reality then you do not belong, and life will go on its way without you and the reconciling love of God, will falter for the moment at least.

Martin Buber in his book *Between Man and Man* talks about The Unique One (God) and The Single One (You, I, Us as individuals) — the relationship between the I and Thou.

Speaking of The Single One in Responsibility he writes: "It cannot be that the relation of the human person to God is established by the subtraction of the world. The single one must therefore take his world, what of the world is extended and entrusted to him in his life, without any reduction into his life's devotion; he must let his world partake unabated of its essentiality. It cannot be that the Single One finds God's hands when he stretches his hands out and away beyond creation. He must put his arms round the vexatious world, whose true name is creation; only then do his fingers reach the realm of lighting and grace.

— He must face the hour which approaches him, the biographical and historical hour, just as it is, in its whole world content and apparently senseless contradiction, without weakening the impact of otherness in it. He must hear the message, stark and un-transfigured, which is delivered to him out of this hour, presented by this situation as it arrives. — And he, the Single One, must answer, by what he does and does not do, he must accept and answer for the hour, the hour of the world, of all the world, as that which is given to him, entrusted to him. Reduction is forbidden; you are not at liberty to select what suits you, the whole cruel hour is at stake, the whole claims you, and you must answer — Him."

"You must hear the claim, however unharmoniously it strikes your ear — and let no-one interfere; give the answer from the depths, where a breath of what has been breathed in still hovers — and let no-one prompt you."

This is what we mean when we speak of the acceptance of belonging —accepting our part in the world; as the world is right now —not as it was yesterday or will be tomorrow. To live is to love. This is to live, and this is to love —this is what we mean; and this is what it means to be a Christian. This is what it means to answer the call of God's love. "Reduction is forbidden, — the whole claims you, and you must answer —Him." God claims you as his own. You are indeed one of his chosen people. A people chosen for responsibility.

Paul Tillich furnishes us the clue to the last thought of this message. Tillich says, "Love is the drive towards the unity of the separated — love cannot be described as the union of the strange but as the reunion of the estranged."

The reunion of the separation. The person who does not love or even the person who is learning the ways of love and relationship is caught in the struggle between reunion and separation.

I doubt if there is anyone of us not caught in this struggle. If you are not caught in it then you are the perfect one, the righteous one and really have no need of God's reconciliation, for God sent his son not to save the righteous but the unrighteous. This struggle sometimes goes on between persons, between husband and wife, between parent and child, and between persons and God. In fact, as this struggle may exist from human being to human being, it also exists between God and those persons.

It is not easy to move towards the reunion of the separation; it is always easier to divorce oneself. It is not easy even to talk about it and certainly it is not easy to find the answer, although the answer is there and is here. The answer comes from one who died to make the union possible, who died to save. Unless there is a consciousness of things and an acceptance of belonging, there will and can never be a reunion of the separation.

In Arthur Miller's play *After the Fall*, we follow the story of one man's search for an answer. Turning towards the play the stage setting is as follows: "Except for one chair there are no walls or substantial boundaries. The setting consists of three levels rising to the highest at the back, crossing in a curve from one side of the stage to the other. A stairway, center, connects them. Rising above all, and dominating the stage, is the blasted stone tower of a German concentration camp. Its wide lookout widows are like eyes which at the moment seem blind and dark; bent reinforcing rods stick out of it like broken tentacles. Two lower levels represent the hereafter with no religious connotation of heaven or hell. The action of the play takes place in the mind, the thought, and memory of Quentin. We pick up at the closing scene. Quentin is thinking out loud."

At one point he refers to "she" — to Maggie who some believe is Marilyn Monroe in the mind of Arthur Miller. In the midst of Quentin's speech, he turns towards the tower, moves towards it as towards a terrible god.

"But love, is love enough? What love, what wave of pity will ever reach this knowledge — I know how to kill — I know, I know — she was doomed in any case, but will that cure? And am I not alone, and no man lives who would not rather be the sole survivor of this place than all its finest victims? What is the cure? Who can be innocent again on this mountain of skulls? I tell you what I know! My brothers died here." He is seeking desperately for an answer. Staring, seeing his vision, he speaks again:

"And that, that's why I wake each morning like a boy — even now, even now! I swear to you, there's something in me that could dare to love this world again! — Is the knowing all? To know, and even happily that we meet unblessed; not in some garden of wax fruit and painted trees, that lie of Eden, but after, after the Fall, after many, many deaths. Is the knowing all? And the wish to kill is never killed, but with some gift of courage one may look into its face when it appears, and with a stroke of love — as to an idiot in the house — forgive it; and again and again — forever?"

"Who can be innocent again?" But after, After the Fall, beyond the boundaries of Eden, beyond the tremendous complexities of life, beyond our inattention and lack of awareness, beyond our personal fears and prejudices, beyond our lack of compassion and action, beyond our complacency and apathy, even beyond our guilt, "after many, many deaths," is the forgiveness of love.

Beyond the finite existence of humankind is Life — the abundant Life of Jesus the Christ. To know that Life is to have that Life. It is to love again and again — for to live is to love. And even though the way back to Eden is hidden from us now. I choose to think of it not as an exile, but rather as God's attempt to make us grow, to challenge our spirits, and to let us learn for ourselves the true nature of His creation and the inherent beauty that there is in life, and to come to know Him in a way that we never could in Eden. Indeed, to discover a New Eden for ourselves and to in turn build a New Jerusalem. For it is in this world, as terribly complex as it is, where we can stretch and grow into spiritual adulthood, and through our relationship with Christ and the Holy Spirit become heirs of God's eternal Kingdom.

"Come to me, all who labor and are heavy-laden, and I will give you rest. Take my yoke upon you, and learn from me; for I am gentle and lowly in heart, and you will find rest for your souls. For my yoke is easy, and my burden is light." – Matthew 11:28-30 English Standard Version (ESV)

Sermon first delivered at Valley View United Methodist Church, Overland Park – Kansas in September 1964.

WHAT IS TRUTH

"And you will know the Truth and the Truth will set you free."

"WE HOLD THESE TRUTHS to be self-evident; that all men are created equal; that they are endowed by their Creator with certain unalienable rights; that among these are Life, liberty, and the pursuit of happiness."

OVER TWO HUNDRED YEARS AGO our forefathers adopted the Declaration of Independence, which was not only a masterpiece of literature but set forth a doctrine that has led this nation where it is today.

This sermon will attempt to show that life, liberty, and the pursuit of happiness portrays a similarity of the Truth that Jesus taught in his brief journey on this good earth. One must of course be cautious for we walk a thin line as we examine the everyday meaning of truth and what Jesus was talking about.

What is Truth? That is the question or should be the question that every Christian should ask him or herself. It is a question that belongs to our very existence. Socrates informed his pupils that the unexamined life is not worth living. If you are willing on this 4th of July 2010 to walk with me hand-in-hand, we will journey together as we move from an everyday meaning of truth and what Jesus meant when he said, "I am the way, and the truth, and the life."

Sometimes mothers will speak softly to their child and at other times, yell and scream out of utter frustration. They sit there in a therapy session and say to me but mostly to the child sitting in the same room, "I just want him to tell me the truth. I don't care what he has done but don't lie to me. I may get upset, but I can take it if he just tells me the truth."

Why do people lie? The fear of rejection. Every child, every youth, every adult will avoid, if at all possible, rejection. It is like a two-edge sword. It hurts. It is painful — especially coming from someone we love - like mothers and fathers. Rejection comes in many forms. A young teenager couldn't wait for her mother to leave the room before she bursts into tears. "She never listens. She never understands."

How can she understand if she doesn't listen? How can I understand or how can you understand if we don't listen? If we are so busy that we have no time to listen, we consciously or unconsciously send messages of rejection to that other person.

We all do it from time to time. A ten-year-old has no time for his six-year-old sister. He doesn't understand - all she wants is to be with him, to be loved. A 17-year-old has no time for her 14-year-old brother. A husband comes home from work and goes directly to the TV. He has no time for his wife or children. It happens every day in more homes than we want to admit. It happens here at church - too busy doing our own thing.

We withhold information (sin of omission). We exaggerate the truth. We tell little white lies or even big black lies to avoid rejection. All of these are examples of truth in its everyday meaning, but this is not the Truth that Jesus was talking about when he said, "I am the way, and the truth, and the life." — "And you will know the Truth and the Truth, will set you free."

The real truth that Jesus speaks of and teaches leads to life, liberty, and the pursuit of happiness. When Jesus, talks of Life, he is speaking about the very core of our being — our body, mind, and soul. He is speaking of your soul and my soul.

"Be still my soul: the Lord is on your side. Bear patiently the cross of grief or pain." – *Hymn No. 534*

Once we make contact with our soul, we come to grips with the struggle of life. We come to know that not all is well all the time. There are moments when we too experience grief or pain. Perhaps that is the moment when we first experience salvation.

Walt Whitman wrote about the soul in his poem, "A Noiseless Patient Spider." It is a very short poem with the first part depicting how the spider marks out the spot where he will build his web and then begins to launch forth his filament. The second part of the poem addresses us for he writes,

"And you, O my soul where you stand
Surrounded, detached, in measureless oceans of space,
Ceaselessly musing, venturing, throwing, seeking the spheres to connect them.
Till the bridge you will need be form'd, till the ductile anchor hold,
Till the gossamer thread you fling catch somewhere, O my soul."

"Bless the Lord, O my soul, and all that is within me, bless his holy name." — Psalm 103:1-2

"I have come that you might have Life and have it more abundantly."

"We hold these truths to be self-evident; that all men are created equal; that they are endowed by their Creator with certain unalienable rights; that among these are life, liberty, and the pursuit of happiness."

"And you will know the Truth and the Truth will set you free." Our forefathers were on the right track. Every one of them, were in touch with God. They knew something about faith and what it means to be free.

Prior to 1776, our Nation was in bondage to the throne of great Britain. We were the child. Great Britain was our parent and like so many parents today, they didn't want to set their child free. They didn't want to give us the same liberty they enjoyed.

As Christians, it is important for us to understand the freedom we have as a citizen of this great nation is not what Jesus was talking about when he said, "And you will know the Truth, and the Truth will set you free."

That was the problem facing the people in Jesus's day and prior to his birth. As people of faith, they longed for the Messiah to set them free. They did not understand that this was not the freedom that awaited them.

O, they were excited when Jesus was born - Mary was so proud, and Joseph, the Shepherds, the Wise Men. Listen to the opening words of a favorite hymn we sing during the Advent Season, and as we approach Christmas.

"Come, thou long expected Jesus, born to set thy people free."

Expectations! They opened their package and there was that little boy. The Messiah had come - born to set thy people free.

How disappointed they were when it didn't turn out that way. Most of the people in that day STOPPED - went on their merry way and in reality, missed the birth of the Messiah.

Listen as the words of our hymn continue: "...from our fears and sins release us, let us find our rest in thee."

Today, many Christians STOP before they experience the Messiah. "For God so loved the World that he gave us his only son." Jesus the Christ came to set us free.

He still comes - every day, every hour, every moment of time. "Do not be anxious about your life, what you shall eat or what you shall drink, nor about your body, what you shall put on. Is not life more than food, and the body more than clothing."

> "Come to me, all you who labor are heavy laden, and learn from me; for I am gentle and lowly in heart, and you will find rest for your souls. For my yoke is easy and my burden is light."

Once we grasp the in-depth meaning of what Jesus was saying when he talked about life and freedom or liberty then we know something about happiness. The pursuit of happiness. Happiness becomes our quest, our search, our mission. Happiness is an expression of the soul. It is sharing one's self with others. It is God's gift, and it becomes our gift to give to others. God is love. What joy! What happiness it brings when we bring happiness to others.

This past Monday, a 21-year-old mother of a two-year-old son born out of wedlock sat in my office depressed, but mostly anxious and distraught because she suddenly became afraid she might lose custody of her son. She needed the advice of an attorney she could not afford. While she listened, I called an old friend and attorney I knew. I spoke to him with this young lady in the room. He would see her the next day. I was fortunate that he was in his office when I called. I imagine God intercedes in ways we know not. I do know that this attorney can be seen in church every Sunday, and whenever I visit the First United Methodist Church he always rushes over to greet me. Happiness is sharing God's love with another person.

> "We hold these truths to be self-evident; that all men are created equal; that they are endowed by their Creator with certain unalienable rights; that among these are Life, liberty, and the pursuit of happiness."

Sermon delivered at Sunset United Methodist Church in July 2010.

WATCH FOR PLATFORM 9 3/4

Beyond our kindergarten faith, is something more.

The Road Not Taken by Robert Frost

Two roads diverged in a yellow wood,
And sorry I could not travel both
And be one traveler, long I stood
And looked down one as far as I could
To where it bent in the undergrowth;

Then took the other, as just as fair,
And having perhaps the better claim,
Because it was grassy and wanted wear;
Though as for that the passing there
Had worn them really about the same,

And both that morning equally lay
In leaves no step had trodden black
Oh, I kept the first for another day!
Yet knowing how way leads on to way,
I doubted if I should ever come back.

I shall tell be telling this with a sigh
Somewhere ages and ages hence:
Two roads diverged in a wood, and I—
I took the one less travel by,
And that has made all the difference.

I remember using this poem by Robert Frost, in a sermon on a Sunday morning many, many years ago, when I was pastor of Valley View United Methodist Church in Overland Park, Kansas. My best friend, who has since gone to his reward, gave me an A+ that morning. I sensed later it was because he had taken the road less traveled by and that had made all the difference.

I'm not sure what it should feel like to turn 75. Maybe — I'll know next Saturday when that day finally arrives. Perhaps — I should ask those of you who have already accomplished that feat. What does it feel like?

I remember when I turned 50. My family baked a cake with the caption ON TO THE NEXT HALF CENTURY. I'm half-way through this second-half, and look forward with excitement to what lies ahead. I've always tried to let go of the past – knowing that I live in the present moment and that the future is open for exploration and growth. At the same time, I'm very much aware of my history – my childhood and youth, which were such happy years.

I'm not sure when I moved into adulthood. It may have been the moment I told my parents goodbye as I went off to World War II. I still feel my own father's embrace, which he almost held back, because in those days being a man was keeping your emotions in check. I'm glad he let go, and we were able to hold each other for a moment. It's those kinds of hugs that liberates a person – really sets you free. What is that we learn from the Good Book, "And you shall know the Truth, and the Truth shall set you free!"

Watch For Platform 9 ¾ – Now what kind of sermon title do we have here – you must be asking yourself. Some of you know where it came from, and others will learn before this sermon comes to an end. I suppose I've always liked to put a little magic in my sermons – come up with a title that would grab one's attention. I remember choosing the words "Mama; I Just Want To Be Me" – that was somewhere in the mid-sixties when people were searching for their own identify.

Young people couldn't understand why people hated each other. It was a time for one's convictions to become one's commitment. The 1950s were relative quiet years. It was a time of rest and relaxation following World War II. By the end of that decade, existentialism has surfaced across our land – a big word but merely having to do with our existence. Who are we? What are we doing here? What's life all about?

It was a time for such movies as *The Graduate, The L-Shape Room, What's It All About Alfie*. And some great plays came out during this period of history – *Who's Afraid of Virginia Wolfe, After The Fall, The Delicate Balance,* and *Raisin In the Sun* – just to mention a few.

But what was happening on the religious scene – in your church and mine? Small country churches were dying out, and inner-city churches were struggling as people in every city across our land were vacating the downtown area and moving to the suburbs. Suburban churches were booming. The church I pastured in Overland Park, Kansas (a suburb of Kansas City) grew from 37 members to over 1300 in less than seven years.

It was a decade or two of extensive growth. However, the nation's unrest found its way into our churches. Prior to our moving to Texas in 1967, the *God Is Dead Theology* appeared on the scene from none other than our own Methodist seminary, Candler School of Theology, on the campus of Emory University in Atlanta, GA.

Church people reacted with anger and determination. How absurd could one be, to imply that God was dead? They never really understood what it was all about. But for many people, God was dead. He was buried in the rubbish of their lives because they refused to let go of the Kindergarten God they knew as a child. One found the same scenario among those who venomously opposed the theory of evolution.

For many years in my office there hung on the wall a gold cross with the creation story from the first chapter of Genesis in caption.

> *In the beginning God created the heavens and the earth. The earth was without form, and void; and darkness was on the face of the deep. And the Spirit of God moved upon the face of the waters, and God said, Let there be light; and there was light.*

Below it, resting on a set of Encyclopedia Britannica, was a sculpture of a monkey holding a skull with the Holy Bible in his lap. There in quotation, one could find the words of Charles Darwin – Origin of the Species.

> *There is a grandeur in this (evolutionary) view of life with its several powers having been originally breathed by the Creator into a few forms or into one; and that, while this planet has been circling on according to the fixed law of gravity, from so simple a beginning endless forms, most beautiful and most wonderful, have been, and are being evolved.*

I first quoted those words in a sermon preached on October 11, 1959. You must remember that I was 31 years of age and an active layman in my home church before venturing off to school with three children to enter the ministry. I believed then as I do now that the Holy Scriptures were written and inspired by great men. I also believed that while their inspiration came from God, their own historical past played a role in what they wrote on paper.

Those who want to take the Holy Scriptures literally as though every "T" was crossed and every "I" was dotted by God himself or herself, forget about Oral Tradition, i.e., the word was passed down from generation to generation before it was every placed in a written form.

Why is it that we want to forget common sense when it comes to our faith? Is it because we refuse to think for ourselves? Is it more comfortable for us to wave the magic wand, and accept the opinion of others without digging deep into our own heart, and mind, and soul? There is a greater mystery at work within the world.

Watch for Platform 9 ¾ — Why do people wave a magic wand when it comes to their Faith, and become critical of a childlike movie such as Harry Potter? Those of you, who have read the book or seen the movie know what Platform 9 ¾, is all about. It was the platform the children crossed to get on the train leading to Hogwarts School of Witchcrafts and Wizardry.

Harry Potter is an adventure story full of magic and fantasies. Platform 9 3/4 could not be seen by the human eye. It was there - between platform 9 and 10, but you couldn't see it. Harry Potter was scared as he ran to board the train. He was afraid because he couldn't see anything. So it took a leap of faith for him to board the train leading to Hogwarts that morning.

He had more faith as a young boy than many of us as we face the great frontiers of our lives. It has nothing to do with chronological age. It has everything to do with our faith, not some kindergarten faith but the kind of faith that sweeps across the pages of biblical history. I'm talking about the faith of Abraham, Isaac, and Jacob.

I'm talking about the faith spoken to us in the words of the prophets – Amos, Hosea, Jeremiah. I'm talking about the faith of the twelve apostles. I'm talking about the faith of Paul whose conversion experience triggered his own need to share the Good News to those who doubted as he once doubted. I'm talking about the faith of all people of all lands and religions who continue to cross the great frontiers of their own time and existence.

Most of you know by now that our youngest daughter converted to Judaism some fourteen years ago because she fell in love with someone who was Jewish. It was a new and beautiful experience for our family. I think it was meaningful because of what our children learned as 'PKs,' and the openness of their mother and father. This was the reason they accepted so graciously her choice to convert. After all, that's what love is all about. Setting the other person free, letting-go, and you can only do this if you are free.

You really have to watch the chains, especially the religious chains that will imprison you within yourself. Our daughter's mother-in-law spent her third Christmas Eve with us this past year. We spent the last night of Hanukkah at her house. Before she left our house on Christmas Eve, she purposely came up to me and said, "Thank you for loving me." Wow! Wasn't that beautiful?

Watch for Platform 9 ¾ – Take the leap of faith for as we read in

Scripture this morning, "Now faith is the assurance of things hoped for; the convictions of things not see."

I want to leave you this morning by quoting from one of the great theologians of the 20th century. Paul Tillich has been misunderstood by many whose faith will not let them understand his teachings and theology. They simply lack a knowledge and learning of his work. He was preaching from Galatians 6:15 — in which the Apostle Paul was saying that neither circumcision count for anything nor uncircumcision, but a new creation.

In other words, let's stop judging one another, and believing that my religion is better than yours. In the midst of his sermon, Paul Tillich says, "The apostle who was a missionary and a minister and a layman all at once says something is more important than circumcision or uncircumcision." Let us paraphrases the apostle…

"No particular religion matters, neither ours nor yours. But I want to tell you that something has happened that matters, something that judges you and me, your religion, and my religion. A New Creation has occurred, a *New Being* has appeared; and we are all asked to participate in it.

And so we should say to those people of another faith (to Jewish, Muslim, Hindu, Buddhist, etc.) wherever we meet them: Let us not compare our religion and your religion, our rites and your rites, our prophets and your prophets, our priests and your priests, the pious amongst us and the pious amongst you. All this is of no avail!

And above all do not think we want to convert you to English or American Christianity, to the religion of the Western World. We do not want to convert you to us, not even to the best of us. This would be of no avail. We want only to show you something we have seen and to tell you something we have heard: That in the midst of the old creation, there is a New Creation, and this New Creation is manifest in Jesus, who is called the Christ." — Amen!

Sermon delivered at Sunset United Methodist Church in January 2002.

GOD ABOVE GOD

Is it possible that God is more than we may imagine?

I BELIEVE that all of God's children are loved and accepted by him regardless of race, creed, or religion. I believe that faith belongs to each child of God and there is no separate heaven or gathering of God's people following physical death for one particular religion. I do not ask that you believe what I believe but that you so love as you are loved. May you liberate others so you yourself can be set free. In the words of the old Negro spiritual, "Free at last! Free at last! Great God Almighty! I'm Free at last."

It was the end of a mini-vacation in September 2004. I was checking out of a Best Western Motel in Topeka, Kansas. The young woman who waited on me was from India. During our conversation, I told her that I was writing a paper on the diversification of religion in America. I asked her what her religion was! She was very hesitant in answering me. I said, Hindu? She nodded her head in the affirmative and then added that it doesn't make any difference to her. Whatever religious faith a person has is okay with her!

God Above God! Is it possible that the God of the Christian Faith is the same God of all religions? This morning I invite you to examine briefly with me the various faiths of humankind, in an interfaith dialogue, including Confucianism, Taoism, Hinduism, and Buddhism.

I also invite you to examine with me in depth, and as time permits, the God of Abraham, Isaac, and Jacob – to look openly not only at our own faith, but the faith of Muslims and Jews.

Polytheism versus Monotheism! Many or One – If we are to educate ourselves and understand the various religions of mankind, we need to acknowledge that for years polytheism, the belief in many Gods prevailed over Monotheism or one God.

Confucianism (kan-fyu-sha-niz-am) and Taoism may not be thought of as religion per se; nonetheless they both take their followers on a spiritual journey that gives meaning to life and captured the imaginations and souls of those who follow their paths.

Confucius is in many ways synonymous with Chinese culture. That is, he set forth a way of life that has become a giant stepping stone for those who chose to journey with him. Confucius was born in 551 B.C. At the age of fifty, he started his 13-year trek in hopes of improving conditions in China. He was eventually recognized and acknowledged, but by this time he was well into his sixties. He spent the last five years in his life quietly teaching and encouraging others to live with such discipline. So that by their own example and teaching, they would give meaning to life. Confucius died in 479 B.C. at the age of 73.

Taoism (pronounced "Dowism") emerged in China on the heels of Confucianism. Scholars believe was started by a man named, Lao Tzu, born around 604 B.C.

Tao means, path or way. Tao is the way of ultimate reality, and while it is transcendent in nature, it is also immanent. It is the way of creation, the universe – the driving force of humankind. Therefore, it is a way of life, oriented more towards a philosophy than theology. It is quite spiritual in nature as we learn from the following description of Taoism.

> There is a being, wonderful, perfect,
> It existed before heaven and earth.
> How quiet it is!
> How spiritual it is!
> It stands alone, and it does not change.
> It moves around and around,
> But does not on this account suffer.
> All life comes from it.
> It wraps everything with its love as in a garment,
> And yet it claims no honor, for it does not demand

> to be Lord.
> I do not know its name, and so I call it Tao, the Way,
> And I rejoice in its power.

We next find ourselves in India but quickly moving to America, where the Hindu religion is flourishing across our land, from the Atlantic to the Pacific. Diana Eck, Professor of Comparative Religion and Indian Studies at Harvard University, wrote: "Hindus bring something unique to America, a theology of religious pluralism. Hindus come by their pluralism, naturally. The very environment of worship reinforces it. Whatever one's conception of God, whatever one's sect or perspective, one worships in the context of many others. Worship does not begin at an appointed hour and move through a program of liturgies and song and then conclude. Rather worship is multiform and simultaneous."

We find not one God but many, many Gods – thousands of Gods. During my studies of Hinduism, I came across the number 55,000. There may be more or less. I trust the precise number does not matter. For those of us, who worship one God our mind immediately perceives so many Gods as Idolatry, but this is not the case for the Hindu. Each idol is a ***symbol*** just as the Cross for Christians is a symbol, which points to their particular God in a particular time and in a particular Temple, for you will find different Gods in different Temples.

We are more familiar with the word Yoga in the Hindu religion because it is a form of exercise and meditation, which has become so much a part of American culture. The self-realization fellowship was a movement which grew in strength and number over a 40-year period from the 1930s to the 1970s. Hinduism has made and will continue to make its impact on America. One now finds Hinduism flourishing across our land – Boston, New York, Maryland, Chicago, Houston, San Francisco, and Los Angeles.

The mere mention of Los Angeles finds us on the threshold of Buddhism where more than 300 Buddhist temples spread across the second-largest city in the United States. Buddha was born around

563 B.C. in Nepal. He came from a very rich family, married when 16 to a neighboring princess, who gave him a son. Here was a man who had all the material wealth that many people dream of having, but, like so many others, he found his life meaningless and empty. At the age of 29, he left his wife, child, and home to find himself. He sought out the best among the Hindu teachers. During his years of study and practice, Buddhism was born – branching off of Hinduism.

What happened in the Hindu religion that caused this split? Why did Buddha decide to leave the very teaching that gave meaning in his life? First, we need to be aware that six features are embedded in the Hindu religion: Authority, Ritual Explanations, Tradition, Grace, and Mystery; much like the interruption that led to the Protestant Reformation, so Buddha broke off from Hinduism.

Huston Smith in his book on World's Religions described it in this way: "Authority had become hereditary and exploitative. Rituals had become mechanical means for working miracles. Explanations had lost their experiential base and devolved into arguments. Tradition had become a dead weight. God's grace was being misread in ways that undercut human responsibility, and mystery was confused with mystification."

The paradox of Buddhism is embodied in a religion that began by repudiating ritual, speculation, grace, mystery, and a personal God, and ended by embracing them all. Today, Buddhists abound in every Asian land and to a lesser degree in India. It triumphs in the world at large, only to be diminished in the land of its birth. While Hinduism reached our land along the shores of the Atlantic Ocean, Buddhism was moving steadily eastward from India through Central Asia, to China, Japan, and Korea, and then across the Pacific to America.

In the 1850s when Chinese workers arrived on the West Coast, eager to have a part of the Gold Rush in the land of opportunity, which they called Gold Mountain, they brought with them their various religions, including Buddhism. We can travel to Talmadge, California, home to the City of Ten Thousand Buddhas, one of the largest Chinese Zen Buddhist temples in the United States.

We can travel as far east as Kent, New York, in the rural fringe of Westchester County north of New York City. You and I are fortunate, though, for we only have to find our way some six or seven miles from here. There we will find Houston Buddhist Vihara, where we too can visit and catch the flavor of Theravada Buddhism.

We turn now from polytheism to monotheism as we find ourselves confronting Jews, Christians, and Muslims whose religious roots go back to Abraham. Where do we start? As Bruce Feiler in his book on *ABRAHAM* writes:

"He has no mother. He has no past. He has no personality. The man who will redefine the world appears suddenly, almost as an afterthought, with no trumpet fanfare, no fluttering doves, [We read] in Genesis II, verse 26, "When Terah had lived seventy years, he became the father of Abram, Nahor, and Harran." From this a-heroic start, Abram (the name in Hebrew means "the father is exalted" or "mighty father") goes on to abandon his father at age seventy-five, leave his homeland, move to Canaan, travel to Egypt, father two sons, change his name, cut off a part of his penis, do the same for his teenager and newborn, exile his first son, attempt to kill his second, fight a world war, buy some land, bury his wife, father another family, and die at one hundred seventy-five."

That's it in a nutshell — so why did he become so prominent in not one but three religions of mankind? The answer is so simple — because he was the first to acknowledge and accept monotheism (one God). Moses may be more important to the Jews, Jesus to the Christians, and Muhammad for the Muslims, but each finds his roots or beginning with Abraham, the patriarch.

Let me regress for a moment. I'm sitting in front of my computer. It is Thursday morning, October 13, 2005. It is a day of fasting for the Jewish people. It is Yom Kipper, the Day of Atonement, as found in the 16th chapter of Leviticus. Ten days the Jewish people are in penitence beginning with Rosh Hashanah, the Jewish New Year, and ending at sundown on Yom Kipper, which brings forth a feast of celebration following twenty-four hours of fasting. The history of the Jewish people is in one moment exciting for me but so sad at the same time.

The Chosen People, as they have often been called – the children of God, the God of Abraham, Isaac, and Jacob. Chosen and placed on earth to fulfill a certain purpose, and who are scattered among the people of the world. They have been persecuted throughout history, intimidated, crushed, spit upon, ridiculed, persecuted, and put to death.

Allan Levine, author of *Scattered Among The People*, marks this scattering, dispersion, or exile (whatever you choose to call it) taking place in 586 B.C. after Nebuchadnezzar and the Babylonians burned to the ground the Temple of Solomon in Jerusalem. He also informs us that the scattering was made permanent more than six hundred years later in 70 B.C. when the Romans destroyed the Second Temple built in 515 B.C.

History tells us that during the destruction of the Second Temple, 1,100,000 Jews died and another 97,000 were made slaves and scattered throughout the empire. Many deaths and nineteen hundred years elapse before the Jews returned to their homeland in 1948.

It has been difficult for me to imagine let alone accept the reality of the persecution that has flourished throughout the history of the Jewish people. I feel much more comfortable with the Jewish faith than I do with the Muslim faith. I admit that this in large measure has to with my lack of knowledge of the latter.

I grew up with those belonging to the Jewish faith. I attended public school with them and when I eventually joined the Masonic Lodge at the age of twenty-one. I knelt at the same altar and professed my own faith to the same God. There was no distinction between Jews and Gentiles.

During my years in the pastorate, I always took my confirmation class to a Bar Mitzvah service because I wanted them to understand that Christianity bloomed forth out of Judaism.

We were always well received and invited to the Saturday noon feast that followed the morning services. What a great experience it was to attend and participate in our granddaughter's Bat Mitzvah in June 2002. We were so proud of Amy as she led the service that Saturday morning and read without flaws from the Hebrew Bible. I know we will be equally proud when we attend our grandson, Aaron's Bar Mitzvah on August 8, 2008.

The history of the Muslim faith has become more evident since September 11, 2001. It has been the motivating force that has led many of us to learn more about the Muslim or Islam religion. Islam means peace. A secondary meaning or connotation is surrender. One gains peace in his/her surrender to God — the God of Abraham, the same God of the Jewish and Christian faith. Their word or name for God — Allah, is simply God in Arabic.

Islam's founder, Muhammad, was born in 570 A.D. Forty years later he experienced a spiritual awakening much like John Wesley's conversion experience. His teachings as revealed to him by God are found in the Koran, the Muslim's holy scriptures, a book consisting of six thousand two hundred verses.

While Christian haves the "Sermon on the Mount" and the Jews the "Ten Commandments," the Muslims have the Five Pillars of Islam. Finally, we turn to Christianity – the faith which belongs to you and to me. We are and should be proud of our faith. Each of us has a different depth and dimensions when it comes to understanding and accepting the Jesus of History and the Christ of Faith.

I remember writing a theological paper in seminary that I titled, "The Jesus of History - the Christ of Faith existentially accepted for man's salvation." It is only when we come to accept the Christ of Faith that we can in all reality connect and understand the Jesus of History. Our religious faith should be a way of life for us - a path toward the good, the beautiful, and the true. Bruce Feiler opens the pages of his book *ABRAHAM* with these words:

"They start walking just after dawn. They stream through the streets, begin climbing the hills, and drop a few coins in the outstretched palms of the poor. They leave their houses, their lives, their neighbors, and come by themselves or in groups of two or three. Their heads are covered, their eyes down-turned. They are alone. But when they pass through the gates and lift up their eyes, suddenly they are in an illuminated place, a familiar place. They are home. No one is alone in Jerusalem: even the stones know your father.

Once inside, the stream divides. Christians turn north. Today is the last Friday before Christmas, and this afternoon monks will lead a somber procession carrying crosses down the Vi Dolorosa. Jews turn south. Today is the last Friday of Hanukkah, and at sunset rabbis will hold a jubilant ceremony lighting candles at the Western Wall. Muslims turn east. Today is the last Friday of Ramadan and at noon clerics will hold a massive prayer service with two hundred thousand bending as one.

Today is not rare. Jerusalem is a touchstone of faith, and has been since before time began. The legends of monotheism are clear on one thing: Before there was a time, there was water, and darkness covered the deep. A piece of land emerged out of the water. That land is the Rock, and the rock is here. Adam was buried here. Solomon built here. Jesus prayed here. Muhammad ascended here."

God above God! We need to understand this above everything else, viz., that God is above God. He is the God of all religions, and he does not condone one religion laying claim to their priority that they are better than other religions. Throughout history the religions of all faith have been exploited and used to persecute and kill in the name of God.

It is easy for us to judge and condemn those of other religions for their acts of violence but we of the Christian faith have not escaped that segment of life because we too are guilty. We need but look at

The Christian Crusades – the killing of Muslims and Jews all in the name of one we call the Christ. We would say to them – if you don't convert we will kill you and/or at least keep you isolated and imprison you within the emotional and physical walls of your environment.

Our faith does not teach us to kill or hate or emotionally destroy another life. It teaches quite the contrary. Jesus said, "I have not come to destroy the law and the prophets but to fulfill them."

"And who is my neighbor?"

"A man was going down from Jerusalem to Jericho, when he was attacked by robbers. They stripped him of his clothes, beat him and went away, leaving him half dead. [31] A priest happened to be going down the same road, and when he saw the man, he passed by on the other side. [32] So too, a Levite, when he came to the place and saw him, passed by on the other side. [33] But a Samaritan, as he traveled, came where the man was; and when he saw him, he took pity on him. [34] He went to him and bandaged his wounds, pouring on oil and wine. Then he put the man on his own donkey, brought him to an inn and took care of him. [35] The next day he took out two denarii[a] and gave them to the innkeeper. 'Look after him,' he said, 'and when I return, I will reimburse you for any extra expense you may have.'

[36] "Which of these three do you think was a neighbor to the man who fell into the hands of robbers?"

[37] The expert in the law replied, "The one who had mercy on him."

Jesus told him, "Go and do likewise."– Luke 10:30-37 (NIV)

Pastoral Prayer

O Gracious God, we have come again - together as a community of Believers, to sing praises to thy Name and worship thee in the beauty of holiness.

We come, not knowing what to say or even do, as we wait for you to speak to each of us individually. We find ourselves in the midst of summer. Soon summer vacations will end, and the school year will begin anew.

But just for a moment we are together in this worship service to sing praise to Thy Name, to give Thee thanks and asks for Thy forgiveness and understanding, and most of all to once again become recipients of Thy great love.

We live in a world that so much needs the love your Son brought forth some 2000 years ago. Once again, the world is in chaos in the Middle East. The land of your son's birth seems always to be in turmoil, but what about the turmoil in our own lives?

We heard the names of those in need this morning but there is not a one of us who is not in need of your love. Touch the lives of all your children so healing can begin, and peace abound.

In Thy name, we pray. Amen.

Sermon delivered at Sunset United Methodist Church on July 6, 2006.

AGAIN – FOR THE FIRST TIME

"For God so loved the world that he gave us his only begotten Son."

TWO MONTHS AGO, I sat on a park bench on what is called Esplanade Street overlooking the Missouri River. I'm sure it was the same bench that I had sat on many times during my teenage years. I was once again in Leavenworth, Kansas where I graduated from high school in 1945.

Fifty–five years have passed; the buses no longer were in operation, the drug store where I worked was gone, and the high school building had just been closed for its final year and sold to First United Methodist Church, next door, where three of our four children had been baptized.

Here I was alone in the early-morning hours; looking over the river again but in so many ways for the first time. Heraclitus, the ancient Greek philosopher was right. You can never step into the same waters twice. The river keeps on flowing — day after day, year after year. You see it time and again — each time is like the first time for you always see something different.

On this particular morning, I saw my father walking beside me, warning me of the dangerous waters below, voicing to me very softly but discreetly that I must never try to swim in the Missouri River. It is too treacherous with so many whirlpools ready to take you under at any given moment.

I also saw my oldest daughter when she was only nine years of age. I had taken her there to tell her that I had decided to enter the ministry, and we would be leaving Leavenworth in a few short weeks. Finally, I looked across the river and realized that while I was in Kansas, just on the other side was the state of Missouri. I saw all of this again for the first time.

You surely must know what I'm talking about, seeing something again but for the first time. How many patients have come into my office over the years, and on their tenth or eleventh visit they notice a picture or a decor for the first time, even though, it has always been there. I've erred a few times on that one by giving my wife a compliment over a new dress. One she has previously worn, so she reminds me. I'm actually seeing it now again for the first time.

I have experienced such a phenomenon in my reading and studying of the Bible. I want to address that area this morning. I hope you will allow yourselves to get caught up with me in such an experience, so you can understand and share with me the unfolding of a beautiful picture and/or work of art in what we have come to call The Good Book.

As a child, I remember some of the stories from the Old Testament like "Noah & The Ark," "Eli & Samuel," "David & Goliath," the "Wisdom of Solomon," and "Daniel in the Lion's Den." It was years later after returning to the university, at the age of 31, that I re-read stories from the Old Testament. It was like reading the stories again but for the first time.

In my earlier years, I had no idea that the Old Testament was divided into three separate categories — The Law, The Prophets, and The Writings. I learned the Old Testament was a story about a peoples' struggle about their everyday joys and hardships. About the economic, political, and social world, they were caught up in, and certainly about their religious world. I learned about their faith — the God of Abraham, Isaac, and Jacob. I discovered the first five books were considered the Law or Torah in Hebrew — and served as a value system and a way of life for the Jewish people.

The books of Joshua, Judges, Samuel, and Kings are known in the Hebrew Bible as the Former Prophets while such books as Isaiah, Jeremiah, Amos, and Hosea belong to the Latter Prophets. These books help us to understand the people's faith in their struggle between good and evil. The Writings consist of such books as Psalms, Proverbs, Job, and Ecclesiastes. They offer us lessons of wisdom, give us comfort, and often challenging our faith.

Each time I turn the pages of Old Testament it is like reading it again, but for the first time. God chose Moses to set his people free who were held in bondage by the Egyptians, crying out to them, "Let my people go."

God is still imploring us to listen. After I left prison service at the United States Penitentiary, Leavenworth, Kansas and found myself as a parish minister, I started writing a book, which is yet to be finished. I gave it a simple title, *Out of a Prison to a Prison House*. I saw so many people in those early days that were very active within the church but still in bondage.

They were very religious; attending church every Sunday, actively involved in church life, but completely oblivious to what was going on in their world. The Bible, for them, were events that happened several thousand years ago. And in which, there was little they could relate to in what was going on in the present moment.

The Bible comes alive for us only as we allow ourselves to become a part of that historical narrative which set the initial course for where we are today. It parallels our very existence for our own nation is much like the nation Israel when the prophets of old echoed their voices of proclamation.

Vision of the Plumb Line

[7] Thus He showed me: Behold, the Lord stood on a wall made with a plumb line, with a plumb line in His hand. [8] And the Lord said to me, "Amos, what do you see?"

And I said, "A plumb line."

Then the Lord said:

> "Behold, I am setting a plumb line
> In the midst of My people Israel;

I will not pass by them anymore.
The high places of Isaac shall be desolate,
And the sanctuaries of Israel shall be laid waste.
I will rise with the sword against the house of Jeroboam."

Amos prophesied to people enjoying wealth and prosperity but neglecting those who were in need. Our own nation spends millions of dollars investigating each other's political party while there is no money for prescription drugs with those on Medicare. At one point in his utterance, Amos says:

[18] Woe to you who desire the day of the Lord! For what good is the day of the Lord to you? It will be darkness, and not light. – Amos 5:18 (NKJV)

Could we paraphrase that today by saying: Why are you waiting for the Second Coming? Why would you look for and have the Messiah return? This would be of no avail to you, but let justice roll down like waters and righteousness like an ever-flowing stream.

Again – For The First Time!

On Father's Day of this year, I found myself with my two sons, attending church together, breaking bread together, and sharing our lives with one another. My oldest son gave me a book, which I had not previously read. It was by Marcus J. Borg, Professor of Religion and Culture at Oregon State University. He simply titled it, *Meeting Jesus Again For The First Time*. Now you know the spin-off for the title of my sermon.

What impressed me so much about his book is the affirmation he gave me in my understanding of Jesus' life and ministry. Remember the words of Paul, "When I was a child, I spoke like a child, I thought like a child, I reasoned like a child; when I became an adult, I put an end to childish ways."

We have a granddaughter who just turned eleven. We have noticed of late that she acts more like a young lady than a child. Her roles are shifting just as her thought pattern and reasoning ability is shifting.

As a child, I took Christ's miracle stories to be just that – a bit of magic like we read about in the Harry Potter books. I'm on my fourth one. Which ones are you reading? But then — perhaps not, after all magic is for kids. As a kid I thought it was really cool that Jesus healed the leper or healed the woman who was hemorrhaging or the blind man from birth.

I had some idea what it must be like not to see, but I really had no idea what leprosy was and certainly had no knowledge about the woman had who was hemorrhaging.

Reading the book *Meeting Jesus Again For The First Time* affirmed my belief that Jesus was not a religious person but a spirit person. There is a lot of difference between the two for a religious person may belong to an institutional church be he/she a Christian, Jew, Muslim, Buddhist, etc. A spirit person is someone who cares about humanity without taking into account their religious or nonreligious beliefs. Jesus was a spirit person, which means he was also a compassionate person.

My life's journey has been full; my cup has run over many times. I have been blessed because I have touched the lives of so many beautiful people. Two months ago when I made my trek to Leavenworth, I rented a bike for the first time. I rode up and down those hills, just as I had when I was delivering prescriptions as a teenager.

I soon learned that those hills were much more difficult to climb in my present state of being than 60 years ago. My bike then was not a 12 speed, but multiple speeds, depending on how fast I pedaled. Those were the days, when old people had no means of transportation or not enough gas in their car. During World War II, they rationed gas. People might be too sick to leave their home, so they waited patiently and gratefully for you to deliver their medicine.

I remember my years in O.R. in the VA Hospital in Leavenworth, trying to calm and assure the pre-op patients that he/she would be okay. And my years of prison service found me interacting with criminals who were still children of God in spite of their offense. My latest gift was given to me two years ago when I was asked to work with sex offenders.

Our last session before Christmas, this past year found me putting two chairs in the middle of the room. One by one; I would have a member within the group sit in one of the chairs, while I was in the other. I would take three or four minutes to say positive things to the person and would end by saying, "I love you." A seventy-four-year-old Hispanic was so emotionally overcome. He said this is the first time I have been told that someone loves me since I committed my offense.

My favorite story in the Bible was the one read in Scripture this morning. As a child and even a teenager I thought that was really neat – spending all the money his father gave him, and then head for home. That's what a lot of young people do today. They move out – find they can't make it – and move back home.

There is a vast difference though between youth today and the prodigal son. Something very unusual happened to this young man. He came to himself. Now what does that mean? It means he turned around. He was converted — that's what conversion means — to turn around.

His father loved him so much that he set him free – even giving him his inheritance. It is often very painful to let our children go. We tend to hang on to them long after they are gone. We still want to tell them what to do and how to live their lives. The Father of the prodigal son let him go.

He wasn't even sure where his son had gone. He didn't know what happened to him, or that he had lost all his money. He only knew he loved him. His love and compassion so great; that he ran towards him – embracing him and kissing him.

The father threw a celebration because he was elated. He gave his son the best robe they could find, a ring on his hand, and shoes on his feet. Then they killed the fatted calf, so they would eat and make merry.

What a celebration! Why?

Because… "This, my son, was lost and now is found."

There are so many people lost out "there" in the world. We need to have compassion on them. This is our calling, our ministry.

"For God so loved the world that he gave us his only Son."

This is God's gift to us, that we might love, even as we are loved.

These two commandments I give to you: "That you love the Lord God with all your hearts, and with all your soul, and with all your mind. And a second is like unto it that you love your neighbor as yourself."

Amen.

Sermon delivered at Sunset United Methodist Church in July 2000.

EVERLASTING LIFE – A PARADIGM SHIFT

"Earth's the right place for love; I don't know where it's likely to go better."

EVERLASTING LIFE — A Paradigm Shift! We know something about everlasting life. We read it about it in the Good Book. We hear about it on the radio and from TV evangelists. We hear about from the pulpit – from this pulpit and pulpits throughout the world. It is a part of our faith – that life does not end with one's physical death but lasts forever. But what do we know about a paradigm shift?

This was a term used by Thomas Kuhn in his 1962 book, *The Structure of Scientific Revolutions*, to describe the process and result from a change in basic assumptions within the ruling theory of science. During these past 40 years, it has often been used in non–systematic areas to describe a major change in certain thought patterns – replacing the former way of thinking or organizing with a radically different way of thinking or organizing. I'm using it this morning primarily as a metaphor as I invite you to join me in taking a look at Everlasting Life in a varied light and moving away from the traditional view; although, I imagine, that most of you have given thought to this view many times without ever realizing it.

Everlasting Life – A Paradigm Shift!

A young man was checking me out at the super market recently. Noticing his name plate and having majored in philosophy during my college years it came at me like a bolt of lightning. Socrates – I never knew anyone in all these years who was named after the great philosopher. I asked, if he knew what Socrates said just before he drank hemlock. His non–verbal response indicated he didn't know what I was talking about but at the same time begged me to tell him. Socrates, said, "I go to die and you to live, but which of us goes to the better lot is known to none but god."

Is death a better place to be than life? Robert Frost, the beloved poet, didn't think so when he wrote in his poem "Birches," that even though at times he becomes weary of life and would like to get far from it all. Hoping that no fate will willfully misunderstand him, or half-grant what he wishes and then wrest him away, not to return. In his own words, he says:

> Earth's the right place for love;
> I don't know where it's likely to go better.
> I'd like to go by climbing a birch tree.
> And climb black branches up a snow–white trunk
> Toward haven, till the tree could bear no more,
> But dipped its top and set me down again.
> That would be good both going and coming back.
> One could do worse than be a swinger of birches.

I'm with Frost, for I believe that life is better than death. I don't get excited or turned on by some of our traditional hymns such as "In The Garden," or "Swing Low, Sweet Chariot," although I like the beat of the latter. I'm simply not ready for a band of angels to come and carry me home. I've received comments from family members, "Sit down, take a break, rest." Then I think of those tombstones that have the caption, "Eternal Rest" and think I will have plenty of time to rest when this life ends.

I'm a theologian. We all are but I spent three years in seminary studying about God — that's what theology is all about. As I mentioned earlier, my college years found me majoring in philosophy. My main courses in seminary focused on theology — Rudolph Bultmann, Soren Kierkegaard, Paul Tillich, Karl Barth, and Dietrich Bonhoeffer.

I have read and studied so many different schools of thought. I still struggle with some of my beliefs and concepts of everlasting life. Every one of you holds your own beliefs and images formed in your mind of what life is going to be like after death. Still, you don't know any more than I know because it is a mystery. If it wasn't a mystery, if we actually knew, we wouldn't need faith, would we?

Everlasting Life – A Paradigm Shift! So let's move away from what we do not know to what we know. This doesn't mean that you must discard your current beliefs or thoughts concerning life after death. I'm simply asking you to shift gears – move with me in looking at everlasting life with a new vision, a new pair of lenses.

I think now of that great hymn, "For all the saints, who from their labors rest, who thee by faith before the world confessed, thy name, O Jesus, be forever blest. Alleluia, Alleluia, O blest communion, fellowship divine! We feebly struggle, they in glory shine; yet all are one in thee, for all are thine. Alleluia, Alleluia"!

I think now of all the saints from this church alone, whom I have come to know and love these past 33 years. I could name them, but my list would be different from yours. We remember them, don't we? I think of those from Pasadena Blvd. United Methodist Church that I knew over the years. They're gone now but are they really gone? This is the paradigm shift – their lives are everlasting for they dwell within our hearts. There are times when they seem to be, so much a part of us that they are alive within us.

A 12-year-old girl whose grandfather had died was struggling with his death. She went searching for him in the following poem.

> I ran,
> Searching, searching.
> grandpa,
> Where are you?
> Slump against the wall,
> Let the warm tear
>
> Roll down my swollen cheek.
> Let it fall onto
> The frozen plum
> In my shaking hand.
> Where have you gone?
> Inside your heart,
> My love,

A soft voice said, Inside.
That's where.

As I stood before this congregation three weeks ago with all the other Veterans – I was emotionally moved. I actually found myself holding back the tears. I remember that my father was so proud to be a Veteran of WWI, and how his handshake moved to an embrace when he told me good-bye as I joined the Army in WW II.

I was fortunate, because after the war, my father and I, became close friends. He worked with me through the summer and fall of 1956 in building our first new home. We were both employed at the Federal Prison in Leavenworth, Kansas, and we asked and were given the evening shift. So we could spend every morning as well as our days off working on the house. I can still see him – he is as much part of me today, as he was then.

I think of my wife's father, who on his 100th birthday set there in his chair, answering questions one after another as posed by his grandchildren. He is still a part of our lives, and the lives of our children (his grandchildren) and his great–grandchildren.

I think of so many others who have gone to their reward but still linger here – inside of me. Many of you have lost your parents as I have and some of you have lost sons and daughters. His or her life is everlasting, isn't it? They still live within you.

The recent death of Ken Lay, former CEO of Enron, brought out the good in this man. He made some very wrong choices – intentionally, but more unintentionally. Those wrong choices impacted many lives. There is not one of us who have not at one time or other made mistaken choices. We can so easily judge each other, but God sent his Son into the world – not to judge the world, but that the world through Him might be saved.

Do not be quick to judge or expect others to believe what you believe. Do not be anxious about tomorrow, for tomorrow will take care of itself. Do not fear death but instead enjoy life. If you choose to be afraid and anxious that's okay, but it becomes your choice. It is not good for you, physically or emotionally.

Nicodemus was told not to marvel that Jesus said to him, "You must be born anew. The wind blows where it wills, and you hear the sound of it, but you do not know whence it comes or whither it goes', so it is with everyone who is born of the spirit." Allow the spirit to touch you, heal you, and make you whole. You too will feel the spirit of those you loved from yesterday and yesteryears.

Everlasting Life – A Paradigm Shift! And always remember that your life is everlasting for after you leave this good earth, you will continue forever in the hearts and minds and souls of your friends, your children, and your children's children.

Amen.

Pastoral Prayer

Father God, another week has come and gone since we last gathered in this place, at this time. There is so much to say but words seem so inadequate in trying to express our thoughts and feelings.

We ponder – contemplate over a few or many happenings that have touched each of our lives this past week. We know there is joy to be found among us for just two days ago a young couple told me there were going to be married in October. Another couple — much older — came to their counseling session this week and after nearly deciding to split, they announced they wanted to save their marriage. It was such a blessing to hear such good news.

We also know there has been hurt and pain — destruction and death. So many more have died in the Middle East — each side praying to their own God and somehow forgetting that the other side really has the same God.

Are we even aware that it is possible the person sitting next to us or in front or in back is emotionally hurting because a friend or a family member is very sick or near death? May we remember that the names read this morning are more than just names — they are persons, which are loved and need our prayers! Reach down, Father, now — in this moment of time, and let Thy spirit come.

In Thy name, we pray. Amen.

Sermon delivered at Sunset United Methodist Church in July 2006.

LET MY PEOPLE GO

"I have come that you might have life and have it more abundantly."

"WHEN IN THE COURSE of human events it becomes necessary for one people to dissolve the political bands which have connected them with another and to assume among the powers of the earth, the separate and equal station to which the Laws of Nature and of Nature's God entitle them, a decent respect to the opinions of mankind requires that they should declare the causes which impel them to the separation.

We hold these truths to be self-evident, that all men are created equal, that they are endowed by their Creator with certain unalienable Rights, that among these are Life, Liberty and the pursuit of Happiness."

THESE WORDS as we know or should know are the opening words found in the *Declaration of Independence* written 233 years ago. I immediately perceived a parallel between what was happening in 1776 and the events as recorded in Biblical history when the children of Israel were in bondage to the Egyptians.

I ask you to look with me this morning at this parallel. Allow your eyes to open but mostly your heart. Do you not see Moses and Aaron, standing before Pharaoh — crying out to him, "Let my people go!" Then let your mind move forward to the third quarter of the 18th century.

Our founding fathers tried in vain to negotiate with Great Britain, but their efforts were for naught. Great Britain was such a powerful nation during this time in history. America became just another opportunity for them to gain more power and more wealth. Over the years, America grew into thirteen colonies.

The straw that broke the camel's back so to speak was the continuous increase in taxes. Finally, the cry from these thirteen colonies to the British Empire was taxation without representation. On June 7, 1776, the Continental Congress met in Philadelphia, where Richard Henry Lee proposed a resolution urging them to declare independence. This led to the drafting by Thomas Jefferson of the Declaration of Independence, which was adopted on July 4, 1776 on what was described as a bright sunny, but cool Philadelphia day.

Great Britain refused to grant such independence, which led to the Revolutionary War, which ended in 1783. We tend to forget about those years and focus only on July 4th. We tend to forget the suffering and the loss of lives. This is so true for every war. We forget the hardships, the pain, the anguish and distress that go with every war.

In many ways, the picture was no different when Moses and Aaron stood before Pharaoh — crying out to him "Let my people go." Pharaoh was just as mean and stubborn as was Great Britain, for he said to them: "Who is the Lord, that I should heed his voice and let Israel go? I do not know the Lord, and moreover; I will not let Israel go."

We know the rest of the story – so many stories – so much suffering before they reached the Promised Land. Their history is insurmountable — their faithfulness to the God of Abraham, Jacob and Isaac. Israel grew into a monarch form of government: the three great kings — Saul, David, and Solomon. Later in history, the nation was divided, and finally the downfall of Samaria in 721 BC and Jerusalem in 587 BC.

Let my people go! We can still hear the cry. We hear it in every generation, in every nation, in every country. We do believe all men are created equal; they are endowed by their Creator with certain unalienable rights; among these are life, liberty, and the pursuit of happiness.

Yesterday we celebrated our nation's birthday, and we continue it this morning. It has become a tradition for Sunset to set aside this Sunday each year, to recognize and participate in our nation's birth.

Our patriotism overflows, our cup runneth over. There are many of us who have served in the armed forces of our country. I doubt if there is one family present this morning whose immediate or extended family has not suffered the loss of a member over these past 233 years.

As I have drawn a parallel between the time when Moses and Aaron stood between Pharaoh and our founding father stood before Great Britain, so there is a parallel between our religious faith and the role it played in forming the constitution of this United States of America.

During the next few moments let us examine life, liberty, and the pursuit of happiness in light of our own faith. Jesus used the word "life" throughout his ministry.

> "I have come that you might have life and have
> it more abundantly."
> "He who finds his life will lose it"
> "It is the spirit that gives life."
> "I am the way, the truth, and the life."

Jesus looked down at the man who had been lying by the pool for 38 years. Do you want to be healed? Then "Take up your pallet (life) and walk." Jesus is not talking about life in its literal sense. He is not talking about our mere existence. When someone asks me how I am doing and I give them that flipped answer — 'Well, I'm still aboveground' — that's not what Jesus is talking about. We can be aboveground, get up every morning, go to work, do our daily chores and still — not experience the life Jesus was talking about.

He said, "It is the spirit that gives life." It is the grace within you – the inner being and spirit who dwell deep within you. It is that unique "YOU," that no one else has because there is only one of you. Jesus is saying to each of us "You are special!" So if you find that "YOU" — that grace within you will immediately lose it. Jesus said to us, "He who finds his life will lose it?"

Life, liberty, and the pursuit of happiness! The word Liberty — what does it mean? You're right! It means freedom. It means being able to do as one pleases. It means freedom from physical restraint. It also means one has permission to go freely within limited boundaries. In other words, I do not have the right to come on your property or cross the boundaries of your existence unless you give me that right.

Theologically speaking, it has even a deeper mean. Jesus said, "If you continue in my word, you are my disciples, and you will know the truth, and the truth will set you free."

You will no longer be thirsty if you drink the water that I give. You will no longer be hungry if you eat the bread which I give. Jesus used so many parables in setting us free. He often found it difficult to get through to those around him and once said that sheep hear my voice, "why can't you understand."

I give you eternal life — take it — it's yours. Jesus wasn't talking about life after death. He was talking about life right now, in this very moment, in this very place. If you accept this eternal life you will be free. The shackles that bind you will be removed. The wall which you have built around you to protect yourself from being hurt again because of what someone has said or done to you will just crumble away.

Once again, you will stand naked but free. Vulnerable, yes – but free. The person who is free is always vulnerable — subject to be hurt again, subject to fall from grace again; but, also subject to be loved again.

Do you want to be loved again? Do you truly want to reach out and love other? If you say "yes" to either one or both of those questions, then you know something of what it means to be free. "Let my people go!"

There is a voice within you — deep within, but it is there. Be still and listen — you will hear its voice. It is a power greater than yourself —

that power you may call God or Lord or Yahweh or Christ. It is your salvation, your saving grace.

Life, liberty, and the pursuit of happiness! Our pursuit for happiness always follows our pursuit for life and liberty. This is the eternal life that Jesus talks about. It is the truth that sets us free. It is never ours to keep. It is only ours to share. A still small voice – quietly saying but with a thunderous overtone — "Let my people go!"

I close this sermon by sharing with you a poem recently written by someone I have known for a long time. Don't ask for his name now. You may receive it later if you ask. He first writes a prologue which provides us with the background and setting of the poem.

The Harris County Courts District is at the northeastern edge of downtown Houston, Texas, quite close to Minute Maid Park. Within the district are several social services organizations, various county agencies and courts, the Harris County Jail, as well as Christ Church Cathedral (Episcopal), and Annunciation Catholic Church. The district includes a diversity of people. It is quite common to encounter the homeless, the hungry, the sick, and the imprisoned.

THE JESUS PRAYER FLAG

this morning, quite early
in fact,
an hour or so after dawn
while walking to my office

I saw a parking garage attendant
in the courthouse district
of downtown Houston
waiving a red–orange
traffic flag
back and forth
back and forth
with the word

JESUS
written there

there he was
waving Jesus around
for all the world to see
he was waving Jesus
like a
Tibetan Buddhist prayer flag
flying in the wind
stirring up the Holy Spirit

he was waving Jesus as a message
as a hope
as a charity
as a blessing
as a reminder
in remembrance
so that we might
wake up and
remember too

if you listened
carefully
clearly
you can hear
the voices
of the homeless
the poor
the imprisoned, on parole
the weary
like voices from heaven
as they too passed
by

saying ...

Come, Lord Jesus

In My Father's House Are Many Mansions

Come, Lord Jesus
Come, Lord Jesus

uttering his name without pause
as a prayer, as a song, as a thought

in the back of my mind I can hear them singing

"Jesus loves me this I know
so the Bible tells me so"
I'm sure it was a prayer
a cry from heaven even,
it must have been
for I heard the voices too,
the voices of angels
appearing and arising
as unexpected messengers
as strangers
and

I think I saw Jesus smiling,
I'm sure I did,
in the smiles on their faces

as I passed by looking, seeing
but staying quiet all the same
not a whisper crossing my lips
not even a small hello

but certainly a smile, and a hint of some
blessing unasked for
grace given freely
freely accepted

a witness to
God's compassion
at work
in the world

the Kingdom
of God
coming closer
and closer
each day

Amen

Sermon delivered at Sunset United Methodist Church in July 2009.

In My Father's House Are Many Mansions

EPILOGUE

Orthodox and traditional Christian churches that recognize and celebrate the Sacraments: Baptism, Eucharist–Holy Communion, Reconciliation, Confirmation, Matrimony, Orders–Ordination, Anointing of the Sick (Healing–Unction), know each one as "outward and visible signs of inward and spiritual grace." Sacraments, in any form, involve an invocation of and an encounter with the Holy Spirit. They offer us a communion with God as "Spirit & Truth" and with one another in the community of Christ, the church.

JOHN 4:23-24 (AKJV) — 23 But the hour cometh, and now is, when the true worshippers shall worship the Father in spirit and in truth: for the Father seeketh such to worship him. 24 God *is* a Spirit: and they that worship him must worship *him* in spirit and in truth.

There is of course a deeper mystery at work here for Christians; one, which involves the *Indwelling* of the Holy Spirit who prays in and with and through us, even when we do not know how to pray on our own. We may approach any spiritual practice such as prayer and meditation, or even something new like YogaMass®, as a sacrament. The intention is to open more fully our hearts and minds and souls to God and in remembrance of Jesus Christ.

Such practices encourage our spiritual formation and help us to grow closer to God, and to see the infinite potential of all things arising from creation. "God is love, and those who abide in love abide in God, and God abides in them." – 1 John 4:16 (NRSV)

ACKNOWLEGMENTS

Ron Starbuck ~ Saint Julian Press ~ Executive Editor

Robert P. Starbuck loved great literature — literary poetry, plays, and prose. He found something in them that was sacred and, which runs parallel to the lessons and teachings he found in holy scripture.

Many of his thoughts and sermons draw upon well-known artistic works of great American poets, writers, playwrights, and lyrists. The works are so beloved that they have become a part of America's literary heritage and adopted as symbols of our nation's cherished values.

These values arise from the abundant diversity of American society. Through the many faiths, cultures, stories, and history of America, and shape us internally. In this sense, these works are transformative. They have transformed us as Americans and celebrated as part of our collective liturgy and consciousness.

They have become works of the people, about and for the people, and beloved by the people. They belong to and are part of America's cultural and artistic legacy. We can think of no greater acknowledgement or recognition of their creative and transcendent worth.

They are included in this book and the works cited at the end, with the gracious permission of the publisher, the author, the estate or family of the author, or as "Fair Use" for non-profit educational purposes, or that may now dwell within the public domain.

ST. JOHN LUTHERAN CHURCH
~ Easton, Kansas ~

On the front cover of *In My Father's House Are Many Mansions*, is an impressionistic art image of St. John Lutheran Church near the township of Easton, Kansas. A special acknowledgment and Thanksgiving must be given to the church as a Christian community of faith and believers. And as family too, since our connection to the community goes back several generations.

This is where my mother, Edna Meinert–Starbuck was baptized and confirmed, and married in 1948. It is where her parents in 1920, and her grandparents in 1883 were married too. St. John Lutheran Church was originally founded in 1880 by German Lutheran immigrants to America. My mother's great grandfather Heinrich Friedrich Weilhelm (Henry) Meinert served as one of the original trustees. St. John Lutheran Church is a place where our extended family still gathers on Sunday mornings and special occasions to worship.

The cover image was created from an original photograph taken by Kelly Taylor-Mailen, when it snowed. Kelly's family has a long history with the church, and is the granddaughter of Austin and LaVerne "Kruse" Potter. She now lives with her husband Russell, in Auburn, Alabama, and works for Auburn University and with the Alabama Cooperative Extension System.

GENDER-NEUTRAL LANGUAGE

When possible, the original prose was transformed to be more inclusive and use gender-neutral language. In a few cases, this became challenging when it influenced the poetic essence and *nous* of the prose. Whenever you see a masculine pronoun for God, please see it as metaphorical and symbolic language. God is neither male nor female, God is Spirit and Truth and Love. Invisible – Unseen – Formless – Beyond All Forms.

WORKS CITED & NOTES

Introduction

1. Brokaw, Tom. *The Greatest Generation*, Random House, 2004.
2. MacLeish, *The Hamlet of A. MacLeish*, Houghton Mifflin Company, 1928.
3. Matthew 22:37-40, *The Book of Common Prayer – Penitential Order Rite I*, Church Publishing, 2007.

The Missiles of October – Part One and Two:

1. Ephesians 2:12-13 (New English Bible - Oxford University Press).
2. *A Mighty Fortress Is Our God* – A hymn written and composed by Martin Luther between 1527 and 1529.
3. A statement by U Thant as Acting Secretary General of the United Nations on October 24, 1962, to the Security Council and in his correspondence to U.S. President Kennedy and USSR (Russia) Chairman Khrushchev. U Thant, a devout Buddhist, was appointed as the Acting Secretary-General of the United Nations in 1961, when his predecessor, Dag Hammarskjöld, died in an air crash. In his first term, he facilitated negotiations between U.S. President John F. Kennedy and Soviet premier Nikita Khrushchev during the Cuban Missile Crisis. He helped to avert a global cataclysm.
4. Opening Speech For Council Of Vatican II – Pope John XXIII – October 11, 1962 – (On October 11, 1962, the first day of the Council, Pope John XXIII delivered this address in St. Peter's Basilica.).
5. Third Assembly of the World Council of Churches, New Delhi 1961.
6. *American Journal of Orthopsychiatry* January 1962 – Dr. Margaret Mead.
7. Cousins, Norman. *In Place Of Folly*. Harper & Brothers, 1960. Published for the National Committee For A Sane Nuclear Policy.
8. Psalm 137 – Revised Standard Version.

9. Hosea 14 – Revised Standard Version.

A Nation Weeps – November 24, 1963:

1. *The Gettysburg Address* by President Abraham Lincoln, 1863.
2. *America the Beautiful* – Lyrics by Katharine Lee Bates and music composed by Samuel A. Ward, first published 1910.
3. *Breath On Me, Breath of God.* Hymn written by Edwin Hatch, 1878.
4. *For All the Saints.* Written by Archbishop of Wakefield, William Walsham How, 1864.

Something More Than Palms – Palm Sunday April 7, 1968:

1. Zechariah 9:9 – Revised Standard Version (RSV).
2. Lamentations 5:1-2 (RSV).
3. Zechariah 10:6.
4. *The Robe* by Lloyd C. Douglas, Chapter V – Houghton Miffin 1942, © 1942, Renewed © 1969.
5. King Jr, Martin Luther, *A Letter from Birmingham Jail*, April 16, 1963.

EDITOR'S PERSONAL NOTE

In April of 1968, my father was only 41 years old. I was close to 16, soon to receive my driver's license and a sophomore attending South Park High School in Beaumont, Texas. We lived in the parsonage of St. Paul's United Methodist Church. The house was located in the blue–collar working–class neighborhood of South Park.

St. Paul's United Methodist Church and South Park High School were one block from one another. The church at Woodrow Ave., and the school on Highland Avenue, were only four-five blocks from Lamar University.

To this day, I remember with great fondness how warm and gracious and welcoming the people at St. Paul's United Methodist were to my family.

There is an important back story here — South Park High School was integrated in the late 1960s. And in the direct aftermath of Martin Luther King Jr.'s death, a group of black and white students gathered at the church's parsonage one evening to learn more about one another.

My parents welcomed them all; they opened up our home to a new generation, a generation that wanted something more. Most of us were only 15–17 years old and trying our best to understand the dark and confusing things taking place within our world.

Why do we hate?

Why is there war?

How can we make the world better?

There is something else I remember too. It is how my father cried like a baby the day Martin Luther King Jr. was killed. And how, at some point, we simply held one another. There are deep memories here, pain and sorrow and great love, which should not be forgotten.

There are small simple transforming stories of humanity's love that need to be shared and treasured. This is one of those stories to be remembered; it is a remembrance.

Two months later, on June 6, 1968, the nation witnessed the assassination of Robert F. Kennedy.

You've Got To Be Taught – June 9, 1968

1. Starbuck, Edna. "Thoughts", © Saint Julian Press, Inc. 2018.
2. "You've Got to Be Carefully Taught" – *South Pacific* – Rodgers & Hammerstein © 1949 – Williamson Music Company.
3. Tillich, Paul. *The Shaking of the Foundations* – "You Are Accepted" – Charles Scribner's Sons, New York, 1948.
4. Dooley, Tom. *The Night They Burned The Mountain*, Farrar Straus & Giroux, 1960.
5. King Jr., Martin Luther. *I Have a Dream*, during the March on Washington for Jobs and Freedom, August 28, 1963.

EDITOR'S PERSONAL NOTE

In June 1968, after the assassination of Robert Kennedy, at age 16 – I attended my first political campaign rally. It was for the Presidential campaign of Senator Eugene J. McCarthy, from Minnesota. Senator McCarthy was not only a politician, he was a poet and writer as well, writing well into his ninth decade.

Something More Important – August 9, 1970

1. Matthew 12:10-14 Revised Standard Version (RSV).
2. "Cryin' to Be Heard," *Traffic* studio album released October 1968. Written by Dave Mason – recorded Olympic Studios, London, Record Plant, NYC, January – May 1968 with Mason – lead vocal, Winwood – bass, Hammond – organ, harpsichord, backing vocal; Wood – soprano saxophone; Capaldi – drums, backing vocal.

Do You See What I See – A Christmas Sermon:

1. Regney, Noël, and Baker, Gloria Shayne. *Do You Hear What I Hear,* – lyrics by Noël Regney & music by Gloria Shayne Baker, 1962.
2. Tillich, Paul. *The Shaking of the Foundations* – "You Are Accepted," Charles Scribner's Sons, New York, 1948.
3. Weems, Ann. "Christmas Trees And Strawberry Summers," *Kneeling In Bethlehem,* Westminster John Knox Press, 1992.

The Afterglow:

1. Dromgoole, Will Allen. "The Bridge Builder," *Father: An Anthology of Verse*, EP Dutton & Company, 1931.
2. Mitchell, Ruth Comfort. "The Voyagers," Published in *Harper's Magazine*, December 1921-May 1922, Volume 144, page 252.

    Ruth Comfort Mitchell and John Steinbeck both lived in Los Gatos, California. She wrote her novel *Of Human Kindness*, as a literary rebuttal to Steinbeck's, *The Grapes of Wrath*.

The Quest Belongs To Each Of Us

1. Schweitzer, Albert. *The Quest of the Historical Jesus* translated F.C. Burkett, D.D. – published by A. & C. Black, Ltd. 1910.
2. Wroblewski, David. *The Story of Edgar Sawtelle*, Publisher: Ecco, 2008.
3. John 4:7-15 – "Jesus and the Woman of Samaria" (Revised Standard Version).
4. Newton, John. "Amazing Grace" – written by Anglican priest John Newton and published in 1779.

To Live Is To Love:

1. Acts 17:28 New International Version (NIV).
2. John 15:5 New King James Version (NKJV).
3. Socrates at his trial for impiety.
4. Tillich, Paul. *Systematic Theology, Volume One thru Volume Three*, University of Chicago Press, 1951 – (1) The consciousness of things, (2) The acceptance of belonging, and (3) The reunion of the separation.
5. Schleiermacher, Friedrich. – *On Religion: Speeches to its Cultured Despisers*, translated, with introduction, by John Oman, B.D. London, Kegan Paul, Trench, Trubner & Co., Ltd. Paternoster House, Charing Cross Road, 1893, Page 36.
6. Martin Buber – *Between Man and Man*, Macmillan (1978)

7. Miller, Arthur. – *After the Fall*, Dramatists Play Service, Inc., 1964. The play premiered on Broadway at the ANTA Washington Square Theatre, on January 23, 1964.
8. Matthew 11:28-30 English Standard Version (ESV).

What Is Truth:

1. Jefferson, Thomas: Declaration of Independence 1776.
2. Socrates: The dictum uttered at his trial found in Plato's writings. Plato. Plato in Twelve Volumes, Vol. 1 translated by Harold North Fowler; Introduction by W.R.M. Lamb. Cambridge, MA, Harvard University Press; London, William Heinemann Ltd. 1966.
3. Whitman, Walt. "A Noiseless Patient Spider," *Leaves of Grass*, 1891 edition. It was originally part of his poem "Whispers of Heavenly Death," written expressly for *The Broadway*, A London Magazine, issue 10 (October 1868), numbered as stanza "3." It was retitled "A Noiseless Patient Spider" and reprinted as part of a larger cluster in *Passage to India* (1871).

Watch for Platform 9 ¾

1. Frost, Robert: "The Road Not Taken," *Mountain Interval*, Henry Holt And Company, 1916.
2. Rowling, J.K. Harry Potter fantasy novels – Bloomsbury Publishing (UK), Scholastic Publishing (US), Raincoast Books (Canada) 1997 thru 2007.
3. Genesis 1:1-3 (KJV).
4. Darwin, Charles. *The Origin of the Species*.
5. Tillich, Paul. *The New Being* - Charles Scribner's Sons 1955.

God Above God:

1. Tillich, Paul. *Systematic Theology – Volume One*, "God Above God," - University of Chicago Press, 1951.
2. Feiler, Bruce. *Abraham*, Harper Collins-William Morrow Publishers, 2002.

3. Levin, Allan. *Scattered Among The People*, The Overlook Press, 2003.
4. Lao Tzu, *Tao Te Ching*, 6th–century A.D.
5. Smith, Houston. *The Religions of Man*, from the Tao The Ching, chapter 25, p. 215, HarperOne, 1958.

Again – For the First Time

1. Amos 7:7-9 New King James Version (NKJV).
2. Borg, Marcus. *Meeting Jesus Again For The First Time*, HarperOne, 2009.
3. 1 Corinthians 13:11 New Revised Standard Version (NRSV).
4. Luke 15:11-32 Luke 15:11-32 New Revised Standard Version (NRSV) – The Parable of the Prodigal and His Brother.

Everlasting Life – A Paradigm Shift

1. Kuhn, Thomas. *The Structure of Scientific Revolutions*, University of Chicago Press, 1962.
2. Frost, Robert. "Birches." From *The Poetry of Robert Frost by Robert Frost*, Holt Rinehart and Winston, Inc., 1930.
3. How, William Walsham. "For All the Saints," first printed in *Hymns for Saints' Days, and Other Hymns*, by Earl Nelson, 1864.
4. Poet Unknown. The twelve-year-old girl's poem.
5. John 3:7-8 Revised Standard Version (RSV).

Let My People Go

1. Jefferson, Thomas: *Declaration of Independence*, 1776.
2. Exodus 8:1 Revised Standard Version (RSV).
3. John 10:10 New King James (NKJV).
4. Matthew 10:39 New King James (NKJV).
5. John 6:63 New King James (NKJV).
6. John 14:6 New King James (NKJV).
7. John 5:8 Revised Standard Version (RSV).
8. John 6:63 Revised Standard Version (RSV).
9. Starbuck, Ron. "The Jesus Prayer Flag," *There Is Something About Being An Episcopalian*, Saint Julian Press, Inc. (2016).

Epilogue

1. JOHN 4:23-24 Authorized King James Version (AKJV)
2. Davis, Gena. *YogaMass: Embodying Christ Consciousness*, Balboa Press 2017. (Rev. Gena Davis – Episcopal priest)
3. 1 John 4:16 New Revised Standard Version (NRSV)

ABOUT THE AUTHOR

Robert Starbuck received his BA in philosophy from Baker University, in Baldwin City, Kansas; his M.Div. from St. Paul's School of Theology in Kansas City, Missouri; and his Ph.D. in Marriage and Family Counseling from Texas Women's University Institute of Health Sciences – Texas Medical Center/Houston, Texas. He served as an ordained Methodist Minister in both the UMC Great Plains - Kansas and UMC Texas Conferences.

He was also a loving son, a husband – married for over 64 years, a father of four, a grandfather, and a great grandfather. And a WWII veteran who served his country and came home afterwards to raise a family and assist others through his ministry and vocation. This book is a collection of essays and sermons comprised by him in his fifty plus years as a Christian clergy, and over forty years as a practicing psychotherapist.

The book's title is an allusion to, and a metaphor for the diversity found in a literary and artistic dialogue that promotes world peace, cultural conversations, and an interfaith awareness, appreciation, and acceptance. Although, mostly Christian in vocabulary, the messages are inclusive and encourage an acceptance of other people and faiths across all humankind. In the end, these words are an affirmation of his faith.

JOHN 14:1-4   Authorized King James Version (AKJV)

Let not your heart be troubled: ye believe in God, believe also in me. In my Father's house are many mansions: if it were not so, I would have told you. I go to prepare a place for you. And if I go and prepare a place for you, I will come again, and receive you unto myself; that where I am, there ye may be also. And whither I go ye know, and the way ye know.

TYPEFACE: GARAMOND – Garamond

The characters and text in this book are set in the typeface Garamond, named for the sixteenth-century Parisian engraver Claude Garamont. The font was originally designed in 1530 by printer Robert Estienne.

www.ingramcontent.com/pod-product-compliance
Lightning Source LLC
Chambersburg PA
CBHW080443110426
42743CB00016B/3254